HUNTINGTON LIBRARY PUBLICATIONS

FIRST AND

THOMAS OLIVER LARK

A Selection of Letters edited

THE HUNTINGTON LIBRAI

AST CONSUL

the Americanization of California

n A. Hawgood

MARINO, CALIFORNIA: 1962

Library of Congress Catalogue Card Number 62-17797

The publication of this volume has been assisted
by The James Irvine Foundation Publication Fund
of the Huntington Library.

Printed by Grant Dahlstrom at the Castle Press, Pasadena, California, U. S. A.

To Alice Larkin Toulmin, granddaughter of pioneers

and guardian of the traditions

of California's living past

The view of the *Harbour and City of Monterey, California, 1842,* which appears on the title page, reproduces the key plan published in New York in 1851 with Karl Gildemeister's lithograph after a water color painted in 1842 by a member of Commodore Thomas Ap Catesby Jones's squadron of the United States Navy, seen at anchor in the bay. The house numbered 2 on the key plan is Larkin's. Other notable buildings depicted are the customhouse (9) and the houses of José Amestí (14), Governor J. B. Alvarado (15), David Spence (16), and Captain John Cooper (20). All of these historic buildings are still standing.

PREFACE

ON AUGUST 24, 1960, I sat for three hours in the great dining room of the Sheraton Palace Hotel in San Francisco, listening entranced to two ladies old in years but young in heart who re-created for me the days when California was a Mexican province. They recalled that one of their grandmothers, a member of the Vallejo family who had married a Yankee trading skipper, had entertained the skipper's half brother at her house in Monterey. Thomas Oliver Larkin, later to be the first and only United States consul in Alta California, had joined Captain John ("Bautista") Roger Cooper, his half brother, in 1832, and remained in his employ until he set up in business in 1833. While Mrs. Alice Larkin Toulmin and Miss Frances Molera had never met their grandfathers (the half brothers Larkin and Cooper), they did know many details of their lives that had come down through their respective families. They even quarreled gently on that summer day in the year 1960 as to who had given whom the smallpox in the year 1834. "Your grandfather gave it to my grandfather and his family. He brought it from San Francisco on the ship," claimed Miss Molera. "Fanny, I never heard of such a thing!" countered Mrs. Toulmin. Details followed of how badly "marked" had been various members of each family. The two also discussed persons outside their immediate family circle; they accused William Heath Davis of being "unreliable" and John Parrott of having a roving eye for the ladies. John Sutter was always sponging, Abel Stearns was an awful old scamp, and they had no use at all for John Charles Frémont and even less for the redoubtable Jessie. And so this amiable turning of the dead into a living past went on. Any historian of California who could have been privileged to listen to the conversation would have been delighted. I was doubly gratified in feeling linked at only one remove to two men in whose careers I was vitally interested. When Mrs. Toulmin and Miss Molera spoke of being brought as children to see President Benjamin Harrison drive into the old Palace Hotel to the place where we were now sitting, it seemed that they were speaking of only yesterday; and, when they talked about their half-brother grandfathers (which presumably makes them quarter cousins), it seemed like only the day before yesterday. In return for the privilege of listening to these two ladies and for her many other kindnesses, I dedicate this little book to Mrs. Toulmin, who arranged the meeting, with the deepest of admiration and respect.

I wish to record my thanks to others who have helped me: the research and reference staff of the Huntington Library, to whom I have returned year after year with fresh demands and queries always cheerfully met and answered; the summer readers there, who have provided sociability as well as erudition; the Trustees of the Library, who have awarded me two summer research grants; the Rockefeller Foundation, which also has subsidized my visits to California on two occasions since my work on the Larkin documents began; and the staffs of the Bancroft Library, the California Historical Society, and the California State Library, who have also given me, on shorter visits, much help and advice. I would like to mention in particular the name of George P. Hammond, editor of the monumental *The Larkin Papers* (Berkeley, 1951-), in progress, who has loaned typescripts and proofs of unpublished volumes and has graciously and most generously permitted me to quote from the published volumes without any restriction. Collis Holladay and his sister Mrs. Helen H. Ord, of San Marino, California, very kindly permitted me to see documents in their possession and to publish the one that constitutes the Appendix to this volume. I would like to thank the California State Library for permission to include the five letters from the Marsh Collection. The Department of Printed Books at the British Museum permitted me to use *The Larkin Papers* before its set had been accessioned. The University of Birmingham paid for the making of microfilms and photostats and facilitated my work in distant California by making contributions toward my travel from its research fund and by granting me study leave in 1956. The many American scholars who have helped me in my task must be given my thanks collectively or a list several pages long would be required, but I would like especially to mention the names of Ray A. Billington, John C. Caughey, Robert V. Hine, Doyce B. Nunis, Jr., Andrew Rolle, and particularly the late Robert Glass Cleland, who helped me plan my project when I last saw him, in 1954, at his Rocking Chair Ranch near Greenough, Montana, where Meriwether Lewis made camp "on the River that leads to the Road that leads to the land of the Buffalo" just below.

Of those who have wrestled with my difficult handwriting and even more corrupt typescript or checked as well as recopied my transcriptions, I should like particularly to mention Mrs. Anne Hutton, of Birmingham, England, and Mrs. Carol Pearson, of San Gabriel, California. For her valuable service in checking transcriptions, I am indebted to Miss Haydée Noya of the Manuscript Department of the Huntington Library, and for their editorial assistance, to Mrs. Eleanor T. Harris, Mrs. Nancy C. English, and Miss Anna C. Smith of the Publications Department. My wife and family have borne with my many summer and not infrequent winter or spring absences from England, and the inevitable chaos of my comings and goings, with cheerful fortitude.

I can only hope that my enthusiasm for California, its people, its history, and its way of life will have suffused the pages, to some extent at least, of this book. "This country (prehaps my hobby)," wrote Thomas Larkin all those years ago. "Prehaps" also it has become mine. With its fifteen thousand inhabitants grown to over fifteen million, it is still as "combustible" as ever.

JOHN A. HAWGOOD

Pasadena, California
September 1961

CONTENTS

LIST OF DOCUMENTS

IV. Stormy Petrels: Hastings, Frémont, and Gillespie, March-June 1846 50

"You will therefore as a Merchant write again to Mr Bidwell and some other proper person to go up the river"
Larkin to Leidesdorff, undated [mid-June 1846]

"Verbal Information reached the Yerba Buena (by the Sonoma Alcalde who left in a hurry . . .)"   *Larkin to Stearns, June 18, 1846*

"I am supprised that you did not informed me at the moment respecting the taking of Sonoma . . . I can hardly believe it and do not understand the affair"   *Larkin to Leidesdorff, June 18, 1846*

"Your two letters come in good time . . . Of course there is some excitement here . . . Its very late, and I have wrote all day"
Larkin to Leidesdorff, June 18, 1846

"In the affair going on, I wish you to charge the principals . . . that no innocent person shall be injured"
Larkin to Leidesdorff, undated [late June 1846]

"If you want any Brown Mantas, 28 to 36 inches wide . . . send me word . . . We hear that their flag is a White Union, red fly and a Star & a Bear in the Union"   *Larkin to Stearns and Temple, June 22, 1846*

"Castro, under pretence of attacking Capt Fremonts party . . . intended to attack the Govt." *James Alexander Forbes to Stearns, June 26, 1846*

"All Comunication between here and the bay is suspended . . . send me a small supply of Brandy or Aguard^te and some Sugar"
Sutter to Leidesdorff, June 28, 1846

"In my last letter I forgott to write you for some tumblers . . . my house is just like a great Hotel"   *Sutter to Leidesdorff, July 1, 1846*

"We are exceedingly in the dark . . . The Northern affair is beyond my comprehension"   *Larkin to Leidesdorff, July 1, 1846*

"You observe there is a prospect of some English men of war arriving. I hope it may be the Case and that they may want a plenty of beef"
Stearns to Johnson, July 3, 1846

"Certainly the Bear goes ahead beyond all Animals in these parts. Should not be supprised to see him here in 15 or 20 days"
Larkin to Leidesdorff, July 5, 1846

Thomas Oliver Larkin, about 1849. From Walter Colton, *Three Years in California* (New York, 1850), facing p. 89.

INTRODUCTION

THOMAS OLIVER LARKIN was born in Massachusetts in 1802, his mother, Ann Rogers, being a native of Alderney in the Channel Islands. After two false starts in his career—as a bookbinder in New England and as a storekeeper, postmaster, and justice of the peace in North Carolina[1]— the young man of twenty-nine accepted employment under his half brother, Captain John B. R. Cooper, who was already engaged in the Sandwich Islands and California trade. Larkin reached the tiny village of Yerba Buena on San Francisco Bay in 1832, several years before Richard Henry Dana was to describe its mist-shrouded desolation so vividly in *Two Years before the Mast*. The following year he removed to the somewhat larger settlement of Monterey, the capital of Mexican Alta California, and was soon to set up for himself there as a general trader and merchant in hides and tallow—the main products of the country during the mission period, which was just about to come to an end through the policy of secularization imposed by the Mexican government in 1833.

In 1833 Thomas Larkin married Rachel Holmes, a young widow, also a New Englander, whom he had met on shipboard during the long voyage from Boston to Hilo, and their son Thomas, believed to be the first native of Alta California with American parents on both sides, was born the following year. They were to have five other children who survived infancy. The house that Larkin built for himself in Monterey in 1835-1837[2]—the first there in New England style, two stories high,

---

[1] See further Robert J. Parker, "A Chapter in the Early Life of Thomas Oliver Larkin," *California Historical Society Quarterly*, XVI (1937), 3-29, 144-170.

[2] See Parker, "Building the Larkin House," *Calif. Hist. Soc. Quart.*, XVI (1937), 321-335.

with a hipped roof but with Spanish-type verandas on three sides as protection against the California sun and with adobe brick walls—is now a state historical monument.[3] He himself sold the house in 1849 when he moved from Monterey to the booming new city of San Francisco, then in the throes of the gold rush. The San Francisco Bay area was also in the midst of a fever of land speculation in which Larkin was an early and very successful participant. After three short visits to the East in 1850, 1851, and 1852 to expand and watch over his business interests, Larkin finally returned to California in 1853 and died of typhoid fever in San Francisco at the age of fifty-six, on October 27, 1858. He was by this time a very rich man, though not the multimillionaire he might have been if he had been successful in all his claims on the United States government, his land promotion at Benicia (the short-lived capital in 1853-1854 of the new state of California), and his speculations in the East and in Europe.

Thomas Larkin at the time of his death was not only one of the richest but one of the most highly respected men in the state of California. But though rich men abounded there in 1858 and even men of high integrity were not then so hard to find as has sometimes been suggested, Larkin had a unique claim on the affection and respect of his fellow Californians, not only on account of his wealth, his open-handed hospitality, and his financial rectitude, but because he was in "every way by far the foremost among the men who won for us California," according to the just tribute paid to him by Josiah Royce in 1885.[4]

Larkin placed California and the United States in his debt to this extent through his activities as United States consul in Monterey between 1844 and 1848. Hitherto-unpublished correspondence of Larkin, while he was consul in Monterey, with William A. Leidesdorff forms the main body of this volume. Leidesdorff was the Danish West Indian whom Larkin appointed as his vice-consul in San Francisco during the crisis that led to the annexation of Alta California by the United States.

---

3 Harold Kirker, *California's Architectural Frontier: Style and Tradition in the Nineteenth Century* (San Marino, 1960), p. 13, says: "Excepting the barracks of hewn redwood logs erected at Fort Ross in 1812, there was not a single two-story house in all California before Thomas Larkin began his building operations in Monterey in 1835." A few pages later Kirker refers to the "creation of a style known as the Monterey Colonial. This was the work of the Bostonian Thomas O. Larkin, who . . . exerted a greater influence on California secular architecture in the first half of the nineteenth century than any other single individual" (p. 17).

4 *California: From the Conquest in 1846 to the Second Vigilance Committee in San Francisco,* introd. Robert Glass Cleland (New York, 1948), p. 127. Originally published in the American Commonwealths series (Boston, 1886).

The letters come principally from the correspondence of Larkin with Abel Stearns (the most prominent American trader in Los Angeles) and with Leidesdorff in the Stearns and Leidesdorff manuscript collections in the Huntington Library. Use is also made of a wide range of other published and unpublished material. The selection concentrates upon Larkin's position as consul and agent of the United States government and deals only incidentally with his business life as a general merchant and trader in hides and tallow at Monterey and as a dealer in real estate in San Francisco and elsewhere. In the letters printed here, some punctuation has been supplied for the sake of clarity, but peculiarities of spelling have been retained.

The role of Larkin in the movement to secure California for the United States and to reconcile the Mexican Californians to American rule, both before and after the occupation took place, has been much misunderstood and misrepresented by historians and publicists. The centennial year, 1958, of the death of Thomas Oliver Larkin was allowed to pass by almost without notice in the great state for which he did so much in its critical, formative days. While the men who so uselessly raised the Bear Flag at Sonoma on June 15, 1846, are commemorated by a monument in bronze on a forty-ton base of granite in Sonoma's plaza, no statue of Thomas Oliver Larkin can be found on Calle Principal[5] or opposite the customhouse[6] at Monterey, or indeed anywhere in California. But for the action of his granddaughter Mrs. Alice Larkin Toulmin in purchasing as her home the house he built and also used as his consulate (but had afterward sold), in restoring and refurnishing it, and in eventually presenting it to the state of California, there would today be no tangible memorial to enable citizens to recollect the contribution made by Thomas Oliver Larkin over a century ago to their well-being and happiness. It is possible that but for him millions of them might never have settled or been born in the Golden State; and that but for him it may well not have today become the second state of the Union or even a state of the Union at all.

It is certain that Thomas Oliver Larkin, a tolerant man and a man who admired success, enjoyed comfort, and made allowances for all the crudities to be found in any fast-growing community, would look upon California today and find that it was good. Whether he would have enjoyed sharing Monterey with "the wild ones," San Francisco with the Beatniks, or the City of the Angels with so many other sinners, is another matter.

---

[5] Near the top end of which the Larkin house was built (see view on title page).
[6] Rebuilt by Larkin in 1841.

In view of the size and sumptuous format of *The Larkin Papers* (of which seven volumes of a projected ten have so far been published, reaching the date September 30, 1848), some explanation is perhaps due of why the publication of the present volume seemed to be necessary. The fact is, as reviewers have pointed out (and as Hammond himself readily acknowledges), *The Larkin Papers* possesses a limitation in that (with rare exceptions) it prints only documents that are to be found in the Bancroft Library at Berkeley. The result is inevitably an inadequate presentation of Thomas Oliver Larkin's full career, for many documents throwing light on that career are housed in other repositories, notably the Huntington Library. The present volume may be said to complement Hammond's edition in several ways. Hammond, in his first six volumes, prints only eleven letters from Larkin to Abel Stearns, whereas the Stearns manuscripts in the Huntington Library (which run to over 12,500 items in all) contain no fewer than seventy written before September 30, 1847, and an additional fifteen after that date, excluding purely commercial communications (bills, orders, certificates, etc.) and also excluding all letters of which there are nonvariant copies in the Bancroft Library. Of these eighty-five letters from Larkin to Stearns, twenty-six are printed for the first time here, compared with twelve so far printed (in volumes I-VII) in *The Larkin Papers*. On the other hand, Hammond has printed twenty-two letters from Stearns to Larkin, but there are no other such letters in the Stearns manuscripts that do not duplicate material used by him from the Bancroft Library. Stearns's correspondence with other persons prominent in the affairs of California during Larkin's consulship (such as John Charles Frémont and Archibald H. Gillespie) is relevant to Larkin's career, and several of these letters are printed here.

The Leidesdorff manuscripts in the Huntington Library contain over five hundred items. While but few of Leidesdorff's own letters are preserved therein, this collection contains more than fifty from Larkin to Leidesdorff, of which twenty-five are printed here for the first time, whereas Hammond has printed only twenty-one up to September 30, 1848, and the earliest of these (in Volume IV) is dated October 29, 1845. But he has printed thirty-three letters from Leidesdorff to Larkin, one dated as early as April 10, 1842, and the others from April 7, 1845, to October 14, 1847.

Hammond's first printed letter actually written by Larkin is dated June 4, 1839, over seven years after Larkin first reached California. The present volume prints four Larkin letters written in 1834 and one written in 1836. There are in fact thirteen Larkin letters in the Stearns manuscripts of dates prior to the first one printed here (that of July 22, 1834), but they are not relevant to Larkin's public career in any way and are therefore omitted, though several are quoted from in this Introduction and in footnotes. One of these mentions his wedding in somewhat casual terms. He says at the end of his letter of June 26, 1833, to Stearns: "Ere this you have I presume heard of my wedding & all its Etc's. Mr Jones made a very fine display on board on the occation. In three months from now if you want Soap let me know. Mr Spence has flour that Don Ant⁰ can get. Yours in hast. T. O. Larkin."[7] An engaging but entirely undocumented account of Larkin's wedding to Mrs. Rachel Holmes is given by Reuben Underhill in *From Cowhides to Golden Fleece*, the only serious full-length biography of Thomas Oliver Larkin that has yet been published.[8] Larkin admitted to Stearns in a letter written at about the time of his wedding that "I know but little Spanish,"[9] yet Underhill has him proudly standing by his bride's side after the ceremony "acknowledging the flowery speeches in fluent Spanish."[10]

   Underhill, in writing his biography of Thomas Oliver Larkin, used the material in the Bancroft Library that has now been systematically published by Hammond, and he also used a certain amount from other sources but not that in the Huntington Library. His Appendix contains the full texts of five letters written to Larkin—one from Leidesdorff (June 19, 1846), one from Captain John B. Montgomery (June 16, 1846), one from Captain John Paty (January 8, 1847), one from Alfred Robinson (June 30, 1844), and one, in an English translation, from General Manuel Micheltorena (October 10, 1843)—but of none written by Larkin himself. The first letter of Larkin quoted at any length by Underhill is that dated June 4, 1839, which is also the first that Hammond prints. Other part-quoted letters are to be found scattered through Underhill's book. That of "February 1846" is misdated by a year, as by the evidence of the text itself it must have been written before May 1845. This error may well have been Larkin's own, but unfortunately Underhill is somewhat haphazard about dates and facts and cannot safely be quoted without careful verification. He states, for instance, that Thomas Oliver Larkin, Jr., was born on April 13, 1834,

---

7 Stearns Coll., Huntington Library.

8 (Stanford, 1946).

9 June 2, 1833, Stearns Coll., Huntington Library. Larkin was married on June 3, 1833.

10 Underhill, p. 17.

in the new house built by Larkin for himself in Monterey, but the house had not even been started at that date. Larkin's letter to John Marsh, of July 8, 1845, is made to appear by Underhill as if it had been written in July 1846.[11]

It is hoped that this collection of documents may serve to correct the somewhat superficial treatment given to Larkin's career by Underhill and to complement the scholarly and indispensable *The Larkin Papers* of Hammond. The present volume, of course, makes no attempt to be exhaustive. The documents printed here represent only a selection of those examined, but the letters chosen all have some direct and significant bearing upon Larkin's career and activities as the first and only United States consul at Monterey in Mexican Alta California. For that reason they concentrate heavily on the years between 1844 and 1848, and much of his early unpublished correspondence has been omitted, as has also the bulk of that from the last ten years of his life. Any adequate life of Larkin would require attention to these omitted documents, only a very few of which Underhill used and many of which Hammond has been unable to publish.

A "career within a career" is also presented here in what emerges from the documents concerning the official activities of William A. Leidesdorff as United States vice-consul at Yerba Buena (later renamed San Francisco) between 1845 and his death in 1848. Leidesdorff, as captain of the merchant ship *Julia Ann* and later as a successful trader, storekeeper, and innkeeper, settled on Yerba Buena Cove and had been a business associate of Larkin for several years before being offered by Larkin the post of his vice-consul. Owing to the slowness of communication in those days, Leidesdorff's appointment was neither officially confirmed by the State Department in Washington nor formally accepted by the government of the Republic of Mexico in Mexico City before the outbreak of war between the two countries changed the status and prospects of both men in a radical way. However, Leidesdorff had by that time long since entered on his consular functions, guided, encouraged, and instructed by the more experienced Larkin. He was to face a local situation at Yerba Buena rather more embarrassing and complicated than that which presented itself to Larkin at Monterey, where the latter's position was assured and his relations both with native Californians and with the foreign community were well established and (with rare exceptions) most cordial. Leidesdorff had to seek the status in Yerba Buena that Larkin had already long possessed in Monterey, but he fought hard and well to secure the recognition to which he thought he was entitled and performed his duties

---

[11] Ibid., pp. 18, 126.

with skill and dispatch. His early death at the age of thirty-seven cut short a career that might have made him one of the great figures of California's history.[12] A reappraisal of the truncated career of William A. Leidesdorff is not called for here, but it is necessary to attempt to show to what extent these new documents shed fresh light on the reputation of Thomas Oliver Larkin as consul and spokesman of the United States at a critical period in the history of California and indeed of the whole North American continent.

Despite the high tribute paid to him by Josiah Royce, Thomas Oliver Larkin has remained to some extent a controversial figure largely owing to the attempts made by John Charles Frémont, his relatives, and his uncritical admirers to assert ex post facto that it was Frémont rather than Larkin who was in "every way by far the foremost among the men who won for us California." While in 1846 both John Charles and Jessie Benton Frémont made references to Larkin that were as generous and appreciative as those of others who met him at that time, they chose in later life, and long after he himself was dead, to belittle him and to cast doubts on his skill and capacity. A characteristic contemporary appreciation of Larkin by a man who knew him well and who worked with him very closely while acting as the first American alcalde of Monterey was that of Walter Colton, who in 1850 wrote in his book *Three Years in California*:

> Through all the revolutions which convulsed the country, he held the post of United States consul, and vigilantly protected our commercial interests and the rights of our citizens. He was deeply concerned in all the measures which at length severed California from Mexico, and loaned his funds and credit to a large amount in raising means to meet the sudden exigences of the war. The Californians, to cut off these supplies, managed at last, very adroitly, to capture him, and held him as a hostage in any important contingency. But the work had already been measurably accomplished, and a restoration of prisoners soon followed. Mr. Larkin early engaged in the organization of a civil government—was a delegate from Monterey to the convention for drafting a constitution, and impressed his practical genius on many of its provisions. He has never been a can-

---

[12] Robert E. Cowan, "The Leidesdorff-Folsom Estate: A Forgotten Chapter in the Romantic History of Early San Francisco," *Calif. Hist. Soc. Quart.*, VII (1928), 105-111, gives the best short account of Leidesdorff's life and estate. There is no full-length biography. John C. Parish discusses the Leidesdorff papers in "California Books and Manuscripts in the Huntington Library," *Huntington Library Bulletin*, VII (1935), 38-42.

didate for any office, and resigned that of Navy Agent, with which he had been honored, as soon as the condition of public affairs would allow. His commercial enterprise and sagacity work best where they have the most scope; they have secured to him an ample fortune. His house has always been the home of the stranger; his hospitalities are ever on a scale with his ample means.[13]

This statement, one of the earliest published opinions of the place of Larkin in California's history, may be compared with a recent one made by Hammond, who writes:

It is proper to note here the key position of Larkin in the conquest of California. His intimate knowledge of the country, acquaintance with its leading citizens, and close relations with the governor and other officials in Monterey gave him an accurate grasp of the political situation and vastly increased his importance. Naturally endowed with courage, industry, and a shrewd business insight, Larkin was better informed about California matters than any one, and stood highest in general esteem. His business activities had frequently taken him to all parts of the province, as well as to the west coast of Mexico. In Monterey, he had often provided supplies for the needy central government, and had even acted as its banker. When he became the consul of the United States, destiny pointed to him as the most important single foreigner on the coast.[14]

Writing in 1886, Hubert Howe Bancroft and his editors were hardly less laudatory. They said:

Larkin's closeness in money matters, in contrast with the reckless prodigality affected by many, prevented his ever reaching in a certain sense the highest popularity, but he was always respected by the better classes of natives and foreigners as a man of honorable conduct, of sound judgment, and of conservative though not selfish views on general topics. He was a man of slight education, but of much tact and practical good sense. Duly devoted to the interests of his govt and of the Amer. immigrants, he had no sympathy with filibusterism, and did not ignore the rights and prejudices of the Californians. He fully believed that, either in the event of war with Mex. or by purchase, the people and local rulers might be induced voluntarily to transfer their allegiance to the U.S. . . . [his] course throughout is worthy of all praise, his statesmanship being incomparably superior to that of the opera-bouffe 'conquerors' of Cal. . . .

---

[13] (New York, 1850), pp. 429-430.
[14] *The Larkin Papers*, ed. Hammond, V, xvii.

He was a man to whom nothing like just credit has hitherto been given for his public services. . . .[15]

Larkin, though an unselfish patriot and an incorruptible public servant, was a hard-driving businessman, and the only harsh things that were said about him during his lifetime by his contemporaries appear to have arisen out of disputes over accounts (as when he had a sharp exchange of letters with Leidesdorff in the autumn of 1847) or when a disgruntled business associate or competitor resented Larkin's getting the better of a bargain (as in his differences with John Parrott over the salvage from the wreck of the *Star of the West* in 1845). On the other hand, a close business association with the crafty and at times unscrupulous Abel Stearns, which lasted continuously for over a quarter of a century and produced an extensive correspondence, seems to have been conducted throughout without a single quarrel, and Stearns—a man slow to praise but quick to blame—is never known to have criticized Larkin in a serious way. Younger business associates, who were often helped in various ways by Larkin, have sung his praises most warmly. On December 12, 1846, when Larkin was a prisoner of the Californians and his life in danger, James Gleason, a fellow American trader in Monterey, wrote to his sister, "My generous and good friend Thos O. Larkin has at last been taken as a prisoner of war. He was captured between here and San Juan. They may carry him to Mexico but we hope not. His capture is a great loss to our country he has rendered important service to the Americans in this conflict. The position he holds makes him doubly useful to the cause. May the fates deal kindly with so good a man."[16] Another young man, William F. Swasey, who served as Larkin's consular clerk during the all-important months of March to September 1846 and lived as a member of his household, said of him in his reminiscences, "Mr. Larkin was a high-minded, honorable man in every sense. . . . He was possessed of a very comprehensive mind, and the very highest common sense. His services to his government, at that critical period of California affairs, were of incalculable value."[17]

When a letter that was derogatory to Larkin's character appeared in a St. Louis newspaper in 1847 signed "John Armstrong" and dated from Fort Helvetia in 1846, he denied the charges against him, and

---

[15] *History of California* (San Francisco, 1884-90), IV, "Pioneer Register," 706-707.

[16] Duncan Gleason, "James Henry Gleason: Pioneer Journal and Letters—1841-1856," *Hist. Soc. of So. Calif. Quart.*, XXXI (1949), 37.

[17] *The Early Days and Men of California* (Oakland, 1891), pp. 39-40.

his friends hastened to refute them. John Bidwell, writing to Larkin on April 26, 1847, doubted whether "John Armstrong" actually existed and added, "Your unbounded hospitality is proverbial in California, and thousands can testify to the falsity of the charges and slanderous imputations set forth in the letter referred to. . . . Your unwearied exertions while acting in an official capacity, are too well known to need comment."[18] Juan Bautista Alvarado wrote to Larkin (the original is in Spanish) on April 30:

> I have seen in the "St. Louis Reveille" of 13th September 1846 many charges against you, which . . . I know to be entirely false. . . . I well recollect also that [in 1840] you desired to become security with your person & property for the freedom of Isaac Graham, Joseph Majors, William Chard & some others . . . and lastly that when the banished Americans returned to California, you maintained the principal ones at your house for months together. . . . When you took possession of your consulate in the year 1843 or 1844 . . . all agreed that your Government could not have made a better choice. . . . I don't know that you have ever denied your protection & assistance to any American or other who may have asked for them. . . . In refutation of the charge brought against you of being a Mexican, I can declare that when I was Governour, I tried several times to persuade you to become a citizen . . . & that you always refused to do so. . . . if your actions with respect to your countrymen be not meritorious I don't know in what they wish to make the merit of their officers consist.[19]

Both General Stephen W. Kearny and Walter Colton appended notes to the official translation of Alvarado's letter, testifying to his probity and high standing. "Any communication bearing the name of Don Juan B. Alvarado is entitled to respect and confidence," wrote Colton. It is obvious that they both thought the accusations against Larkin to be entirely unfounded, though these referred to a period before either had arrived in California.

Three days later that genial, six-foot-eight editor in buckskins, Robert Semple, wrote to Larkin saying that in his opinion the Armstrong letter in the St. Louis *Reveille* was a forgery and making a generous amende honorable for criticisms of Larkin contained in a letter he himself had written and the St. Louis *Reporter* published. Semple admitted:

---

[18] Hammond, VI, 120. See also ibid., VI, 124-125, for Larkin's reaction to the "Armstrong" letter.

[19] Ibid., VI, 132-136.

At the time I wrote, blaming you for Col. Fremont's departure [northward into Oregon in March 1846], so much against our wishes, I did not know the particulars, nor was I acquainted with you. I got my opinion of you from the few Americans which I saw during the winter, most of them sailors who had left their ships without leave of absence.

Since that time I have lived in Monterey, that is, since August last, have had much intercourse with you . . . I do not believe there is any foundation for the charges made by Mr. Armstrong.

Since my first acquaintance with you, I have always found you hospitable and attentive to strangers arriving in town, and have seen nothing in your conduct derogatory to the character of a gentleman and an American.[20]

That other California pioneer who was so conspicuous for his hospitality to strangers, John Augustus Sutter, was always a great admirer of Larkin and recognized in the solid Yankee trader and consul qualities of stability and probity that the mercurial German-Swiss did not himself possess. On July 22, 1845, he wrote to Larkin a long account of his plans and his frustrations and enclosed a list of forty-one items wanted at Fort Helvetia. He added wistfully, "I wish you could come here and convince yourself of the whole situation. I looke upon you as the only person in this Country who assist and encourage enterprise. . . . Dr. Marsh is the badest of all. He give the Grog for furs and robed me in this Manner of a large Amount."[21]

Another long-term Larkin correspondent and enthusiast, Faxon Dean Atherton, wrote on August 10, 1843, from Valparaíso, "I have shewn both your long epistles to Padre Short, who says you know more of California and its inhabitants than any one else there. . . . Wilson says you will be the richest man on California." Again, on February 11, 1845, he wrote, "I prize your Letters more highly than any I receive from any quarter whatever. It is really quite a treat to get hold of one." He also relayed praise for Larkin uttered in exalted quarters in his letter of December 3, 1846: "Capt Hastings . . . had been in Washington where he met with Amos Kendall Esq. who learning that he had been in California took him to see Mr Polk who . . . among other things told him he considered Mr T. O. L. one of the most efficient consuls

---

[20] Ibid., VI, 146-147. Some observers thought Semple to be fully seven feet tall. General William T. Sherman (*Memoirs* [New York, 1892], p. 83) said, "He was about seven feet high, and very intelligent," but both Walter Colton (p. 32) and Edward Kern (letter of July 29[?], 1846, Fort Sutter Coll., Huntington Library) gave his height at six feet eight.

[21] Hammond, III, 282.

the U. S. possessed." Atherton went on very shrewdly to guess, "I rather think you must have been giving Goverment an insight into the length & breadth of California together with a minute description of its inhabitants."[22] Larkin had (unknown to Atherton) sent to the State Department in July 1846 his long and now well-known "Description of California," to which were appended a list of the missions with date of foundation; names of vessels entered in 1845 and particulars of their cargoes; figures of the public debts of California on January 1, 1846; names and salaries of civil and military officers of the Mexican republic in California; and, last but by no means least, "Notes on Personal Character of the Principal Men," which mentions seventy-five names, both Californian and foreign, and constitutes a veritable *Who's Who* and public-opinion poll of the province. John Marsh is described as "Argumental, hermitical and parsimonious. Power of influence contested"; Mariano Vallejo "As a private person has but little regard for Mexico, as an Officer more"; John Sutter is "Active, well informed but too sanguine. Lives but in expectation of this country belonging to the United States"; William Leidesdorff is "Active, bold, honourable, passionate, and liberal. A linguist of medium talent. Formerly Sea Captain of New York. Influence contested. Decidedly partial to the United States"; William Hinckley is "Of honour and generosity in prosperity. Morally bad in adversity, of general vitiation of character. Of a high family in Massachusetts . . . worthy of being a better man"; and Juan Alvarado is "For a Californian a man of the best general knowledge, information, and talents, mild in demeanour but violently disposed when under the effect of inebriation."[23]

Unfortunately these valuable documents took more than a year to reach Washington, D.C., being dispatched on July 20, 1846, and received in the State Department only on August 17, 1847. But even before getting them, James Buchanan had written to Larkin (on January 13, 1847), "you shall continue, at least for the present, as Confidential Agent, in the Californias. . . . Your services in this character have heretofore been valuable & are justly appreciated; and they may be of great consequence hereafter." Buchanan then went on to inform Larkin that one of his drafts claiming expenses had been disallowed, for "I have known no instance in which Clerk hire has been allowed to a confidential agent."[24] As Larkin's "Description" and "Notes" dispatched on July 20, 1846, extended to over ten thousand words, this

---

22 Ibid., II, 31-32; III, 33; V, 290.
23 Ibid., IV, 303-334.
24 Ibid., VI, 6.

was a harsh decision indeed. In addition he had employed William Swasey to put these documents into final shape and to fair-copy them.

One man who owed a great deal to Thomas Larkin during his career was Archibald H. Gillespie, of the United States Marine Corps. His views on Larkin, as expressed in his letters to the Secretary of the Navy, were strangely ambivalent. His first impression, on April 18, 1846, just after he had reached Monterey for the first time, was entirely favorable. He wrote, "I am happy to inform the Department, that I find our Consul, a gentleman entirely different from what I anticipated and every way worthy of the confidence reposed in him; and occupies a position here, which has enabled him to protect the interest of our Countrymen with all the zeal his patriotism inspires, and his good judgement would dictate. I am sorry however to learn, that he thought of resigning the Consulship, in consequence of his bills having been protested, and the allowance made to him by the Department being so small, as to subject him to serious loss. . . ." But by July 25 he had for some reason changed his views, ostensibly because he thought Larkin too partial to James Alexander Forbes, the British vice-consul at Yerba Buena (to whom he, Gillespie, had taken a violent dislike), but also perhaps because he had heard that Larkin was critical of the part that he and Frémont had played in the Bear Flag affair. At any rate,

> I stated to Mr Larkin, that the indifference he attributed to the English V. Consul was contrary to the character of an Englishman, and particularly, one like Mr Forbes, who is indebted to his Government for raising him from the dregs of life, and giving him the position he now occupies in Society. From what I had heard of Mr Larkin's conduct in the country, and every act of his life either public or private being so entirely governed by his own Selfish views, my confidence in his patriotism was very much shaken. . . . at a moment so interesting and important to the United States, he preferred his private to public interests, and to all appearance, was willing to allow the Country to pass into other hands, notwithstanding he had warned Our Government of the danger of European interference.[25]

All this because Larkin, who knew Forbes well, was prepared to accept the latter's word (which later was to be fully validated) that he would be happy to live in California under the American flag, and because Larkin did not hasten to Santa Barbara, as Gillespie had urged he

[25] "Gillespie and the Conquest of California from Letters Dated February 11, 1846, to July 8, 1848, to the Secretary of the Navy," introd. George W. Ames, Jr., *Calif. Hist. Soc. Quart.*, XVII (1938), 137, 279-280.

should, to attend the junta there (which in fact was—as Larkin had suspected—never to meet). The hot-headed marine lieutenant's strictures on Larkin were uncalled-for and are demonstrably unfair.

Another and more famous revision of a favorable early opinion of Larkin—amply demonstrated to be false by historian after historian, beginning with the Hittells and Royce—is the impression that John and Jessie Frémont sought to propagate in the pathmarker's memoirs. Although both the Frémonts had more than once thanked Larkin for his kindness and hospitality during the crisis of 1846, and although Frémont at the time had expressed his appreciation of the services rendered by Larkin to the American cause, they embarked upon a strange policy of denigration and character assassination directed at the former consul forty years after the events concerned and long after he was dead. While references to Larkin in the published memoirs themselves are somewhat noncommittal (and nowhere derogatory), and while Benton and Frémont had used Larkin's reports to the State Department extensively in preparing the latter's defense in the court-martial proceedings of 1848,[26] Frémont told Josiah Royce when he was preparing his history of California that it was "entirely a novel thing that Larkin should have had any important part in all this business."[27] Jessie Frémont had written to Larkin on July 24, 1846, "I am very happy that a safe opportunity has presented itself, for sending you my warmest thanks for your hospitality and kindness to Mr. Frémont. Mr. Buchanan sent me all your private despatches, which shew me how much you risked in your generous kindness to him. It is hardly possible to tell you with how much gratitude his family & mine especially my Father and myself we think and speak of you."[28] Yet in 1884 she told Royce that "Mr. Buchanan would never have dreamed of entrusting such a plan [the peaceable adhesion of Alta California to the United States] to a man of the imperfect education and small experience of Consul Larkin." Royce, who had in his pocket a copy of Buchanan's instructions of September 17, 1845, appointing Larkin his secret agent, tried to get the Frémonts to retract this unfavorable view of Larkin, but without effect. ". . . the good Jessie sat calm and sunny and benevolent in her easy chair; but alas, he [General Frémont] lied, lied unmistakably, unmitigatedly, hopelessly" was Royce's judgment of the issue.[29]

---

[26] In the National Archives of the U.S., the Index, Despatches from Consuls, No. 5, pp. 295-297, lists the Larkin dispatches called for by them.

[27] Royce, pp. 116-117.

[28] Hammond, V, 166.

[29] Royce, pp. 93, xix.

Having examined the files of the State Department and the documents obtained by Bancroft from Larkin's sons and from many other sources, Royce not only gave the lie direct to the Frémont's ex post facto story, calling it somewhat unkindly "the true feminine way of writing history,"[30] but he summed up the matter entirely in favor of Larkin. His statement, already briefly quoted, now deserves quotation at greater length, for nothing written since his day has materially shaken it. Royce said:

> Larkin, the man who, of all Americans concerned with California during that crisis, best did his duty; the one official whose credit, both private and public, is unstained by the whole affair; and who personally, if desert be considered, and not mere popularity, is every way by far the foremost among the men who won for us California —Larkin had not been idle, not before Gillespie came, and much less afterwards. He had obeyed his orders. If he was no trained official and no cultivated man, he was at least a faithful patriot, a shrewd man of business, and a cautious servant of his government; a man well acquainted with the place, the people, and the methods of work that must be employed. As an intriguer, he was distinctly successful, and no drop of blood need have been shed in the conquest of California, no flavor of the bitterness of mutual hate need have entered, at least for that moment, into the lives of the two peoples who were now jointly to occupy the land, had Larkin been left to complete his task. And although Sloat's coming would indeed have found the work still incomplete, it would, without the captain's [Frémont's] utterly mischievous doings, have been well enough advanced to ensure with almost perfect certainty the peaceful change of flags.[31]

Yet General Frémont, having presumably read both Royce's and Bancroft's histories of California, continued to maintain his by then untenable position. In a penciled annotation to the Sloat Papers, to which he had been given access, Frémont wrote on or about March 10, 1886, "The influence of Larkin was well-nigh disastrous to Com. Sloat."[32] It is true that Larkin advised a two or three weeks' delay in raising the American flag during his consultations with Sloat between July 3 and 6, 1846, but only because he thought that within that time the California leaders would have thrown in their lot with the United States of their own accord. He may have been mistaken, but it is interesting to

---

[30] Letter to Henry L. Oak, Jan. 1, 1885, in correspondence and papers of Oak, Bancroft Library.

[31] Royce, p. 127.

[32] Sloat Papers, Calif. Hist. Soc. They were shown to Frémont on or about May 5, 1888.

note that the fire-eating Gillespie expressed the opinion on July 25, 1846, based on somewhat contrary reasons, "that had Commodore Sloat waited but a few short weeks, the Country from the [North] to the South would have been under a well organised Government, free and independent from Mexican tyranny and Military despotism."[33] The Bear, indeed, would have gone ahead beyond all animals!

But this was not what Larkin wanted or deemed wise, nor was it in accordance with the instructions so explicitly sent to him by Polk and Buchanan in 1845. Unless the United States government was pursuing two entirely different official policies simultaneously with regard to California, one through Larkin and the other through Frémont, and there is absolutely no direct evidence to support this premise, then it is my opinion that Larkin's was the authorized, and Frémont's the unauthorized, course.

It is Larkin's course that we follow through the documents hereinafter printed, after the successful trader and publicist of his adopted country had received the blessing of the United States government for what (even before he was appointed consul and secret agent) Larkin had decided was both his inclination and his duty. In somewhat smug but entirely justifiable terms he wrote to Secretary of State Buchanan on July 20, 1846, "The undersigned had anticipated the pleasure of following up the plans partially laid down in the dispatch to this Office of October 17th 1845, and bringing them to a conclusion in the latter part of 1847 and that through the will and voice of the Californians. He had confidential agents throughout the country, who would have aided in bringing the minds of the different Government men to the desired object."[34]

Larkin was no great hero, even to himself; he lived and worked on the periphery of world events; very few people then shared with him the dream of California's remarkable future. He was an ordinary man carried along in the mighty flood of manifest destiny but not afraid to ply his own small but vigorous oar. "This country (prehaps my hobby). . . . We must have it, others must not," he wrote—in his characteristically slipshod spelling—to the eastern newspaper editor James Gordon Bennett on May 20, 1846.[35] By that time to Larkin California was a hobby that had also become his profession.

---

33 "Gillespie and the Conquest of California," p. 271. Brackets around the word "North" are printed in the article.

34 Hammond, V, 144.

35 Ibid., IV, 383.

DOCUMENTS

Abbreviations

S. Coll.—Stearns Collection (Huntington Library)
LE [numbered]—Leidesdorff Collection (Huntington Library)
Ma. Coll. CSL—Marsh Collection (California State Library)

Prologue: California and the World in 1831

JUST a year before Thomas Oliver Larkin was to reach the shores of Alta California, Alexander Forbes, a Scottish merchant at Tepic, on the west coast of Mexico, where he had resided since the middle 1820's, wrote to his friend Abel Stearns in the pueblo of Los Angeles asking many questions about California. Stearns, a Massachusetts man, had gone to Mexico in 1826 and had reached Alta California in 1829. He participated in the revolution of 1831 there against Governor Manuel Victoria, who had attempted to expel Stearns soon after he arrived, and Stearns had the satisfaction of seeing Victoria himself deported. On January 3, 1832, Don Abel wrote to Captain J. B. R. Cooper, Larkin's half brother (a letter from whom was to be instrumental in bringing Larkin to California the following year), that Victoria had embarked on board the *Pocahontas*, which was to sail in about ten days.

Alexander Forbes incorporated the information he obtained from Stearns and others into his celebrated *California: A History of Upper and Lower California*, the manuscript of which he sent to his brother in England in 1835. It was published there in 1839 and soon attracted considerable attention on both sides of the Atlantic. It was the first comprehensive history and description of the two Californias in the English language. Alexander Forbes's chapter on the possibility of colonizing California and the suggestion of John Forbes in the Preface to the book of Britain's "getting a footing in Upper California" commended themselves to the London *Times* (of September 6, 1839) as "well worthy of attention to the English politician." American as well as British politicians took notice of this important book.

1

[Alexander Forbes to Stearns, S. Coll.]

Tepic 18 April 1831

Abel Stearns Esq
My dear Sir

I was very much gratified by receiving your very interesting letter by the Leanor[1] dated Monterey the 23 of Nov[r] last—and I cannot sufficiently thank you for the information you give me respecting California. It gives me very great pleasure to think you will at last succeed in the plan you have in view,[2] which however I have all along thought a most difficult task under the control of such men as you must necessarily submit to. Your perseverance & prudence can only conquer those obstacles, and I earnestly hope y[ou] will at last conquer them.

I have always had a great desire to know every thing respecting California, & by all acc[ts] it is worthy of more wise & more enterprising masters than those to whose rule it is [MS mutilated] This opinion is heightened by the description [MS mutilated] give of it, & confirms me that if populated it would be perhaps the most delightful country in the world. How many Countrymen of mine who are jostling one another for room at home, might live hapily in those fertile but uncultivated plains you describe! The continuance of your correspondence will be truly most interesting to me, & I earnestly beg you will write me by any conveyance that offers. Say any thing without study, any thing about your own labours, tell me how you go to work in any enterprise —if you plow any land—if you cut wood, if you build houses—in short any thing that can give me an idea of the country. Are there salmon in the rivers, Trouts—or what not? What does an ox weigh? Can you measure [MS mutilated] acre, how much does it produce? There is a great mistake in estimating the proceeds of wheat or other grain by the returns from the seed, for this depends on thick or thin sowing. The true criterion is by the quantity of land. Please say some thing of the commerce—what is the weight of a *dry* hide? Why is the tallow of such bad quality? It is the worst in the world. I think it must arise from its lying over & heating in the *rough* before it is melted—it is alledged that they mix the suet with it, but I don't think this is the cause. Tallow

---

[1] The *Leonor*, Mexican registry, 207 tons, master, Henry D. Fitch. See Bancroft, III, 147, 363.

[2] Stearns's letter to Forbes has not been found, and the plan can thus only be surmised from what is known of Stearns's career.

is now here very unsaleable. I mean California tallow. That of this country is infinitely superior. Vermont will make a very bad job of his. How many hides could be got in 6 or 8 months? This is the best article —I shall however have done.

By last accts from the United States which is up to the 10th of March, every thing was as usual, no changes nor appearance of changes of any kind. Not so in Europe. Everything there is topsy turvy. You will of course have heard of the wonderful revolution in France, & of late nothing new has taken place; the Duke of Orleans is King, & the rabble has hitherto been kept quiet but with difficulty. La Fyette has cut the most conspicuous figure in this revolution, & has been at the head of the National Guards who have been the principal actors [words "in the revolution" deleted]. He however has lately resigned, & is said to wish for a Republic, but this will never do with Frenchmen. I dont think they are even fit for a Constitutional Monarchy. Flanders is completely seperated from Holland, & they are now debating about who shall be their King. Poland has beat the Russian Army out of the Country, & wait to defend themselves against the whole Russian power. In short, the whole world is in Combustion. England has even had its *rows* not so much about political questions as on acct of want of employment for labourers and mechanics. The labourers of Kent &ce have taken it into their heads to burn threshing machines, & with them Barns, stacks of corn, &ce, but Judges have been sent down to hang some [MS mutilated] of them and all will soon be quiet.

In Ireland there is a great cry to get back their Parliament & to disolve the Union—this is chiefly promoted by O Connel who has lately been arrested & I dare say all will soon be put to rights. The Duke of Wellington & his associates have been turned out, & a new Whig Ministry formed, with Earl Grey at its head. These are the most able men in England & must do much good.

As far as regards this Republic, every thing is quiet. Genl Guerrero has been taken & shot, and Bustamente & his Govt have no opposition. The finances are as usual in a bad state, & commercial restrictions & high duties remains the same as before. Notwithstanding this there has been a very considerable business at S. Blas. Of the rest of the Republics of Am. it is needless to say more than that the[y are] in the greatest confusion & disorder. Bolivar is dead—I believe of a broken heart.[3] Peru is about to go to war with the new state of Bolivia. Chile has lately

---

3 Simón Bolívar died of tuberculosis at the age of 47 near Santa Marta, Colombia, on Dec. 17, 1830.

changed her gov^t, & at Buenos Ayres they are fighting amongst themselves & reduced to the greatest possible misery.

You asked for a long letter and I am sure you have it, so adios.

Yours very truly,
Alex: Forbes

I. The Flag Follows Trade

July 1834 - April 1843

FROM 1833 to 1844 the newly arrived Thomas Oliver Larkin bent his main energies toward establishing himself as a trader in Alta California and in laying the foundations of his considerable fortune. But he found time to build himself a house, almost the first in California with two stories, and was a pioneer in the use of redwood timber (from Santa Cruz) in its construction. Even before the Larkin house was completed, its owner began to entertain and accommodate visiting Americans. One of his earliest (and least welcome) guests was Hall Jackson Kelley, who in 1831 had organized the American Society for Encouraging the Settlement of the Oregon Territory. Kelley, while in Monterey (which he had reached by sea), persuaded the fur trader Ewing Young to accompany him to the Columbia River, where Dr. John McLoughlin, chief factor of the Hudson's Bay Company, permitted him to winter at Fort Vancouver. Kelley returned to Boston by sea in 1836. His "Memoir" on the Oregon country was printed by order of the House of Representatives in 1839 (House Report No. 101, 25 Cong. 3 Sess., Appendix). That Larkin obviously had no use whatsoever for Hall J. Kelley is evident in his letter of July 22, 1834, to Abel Stearns.

The remaining letters in the following section illustrate in detail the difficulties and frustrations that faced foreigners (and indeed some natives also) who attempted to trade in Mexican California in those days. Constant unrest and revolution made "unsettled times" the norm rather than the exception. The inefficiency and officiousness of the Mexican authorities was vexing, but Larkin bore all this with remarkable equanimity, especially as he was often involved in financial loss as a consequence. The letter to Stearns of December 8, 1842, tells simply and

5

vividly the local effect of Commodore Thomas Ap Catesby Jones's in-
judicious seizure of Monterey seven weeks earlier. The letter of April
18, 1843, is unusual in that Larkin gets away from his business and
from local California problems for a change and comments broadly
and amusingly on world affairs. Although he did not then know it, his
name was already being considered in Washington for appointment as
United States consul for California. His horizon was still almost completely confined to his trading interests, in pursuit of which he paid
visits to Mexico in 1840 and 1843.

All the letters of this section are addressed to Abel Stearns, who was
prospering considerably in southern California as a merchant, land-
owner, and ranchero. The letters represent only a small selection of the
many Larkin wrote to Stearns between 1833 and 1844—although he
said in his letter of April 18, 1843 (perhaps ironically), "I am not a
Correspondent of yours"—but most of those not included are strictly
"business correspondence" concerned with ships and shoes and sealing
wax, and, above all, with hides and tallow and redwood logs.

[Larkin to Stearns, S. Coll.]

Monterrey July 22d 1834

Mr A. Stearns

I wrote last by Mr Leece[1]—who left here two days back, but presume
he will be a month going down. I paid a man last spring to get out your
thick stuff—he disapointed me & I had two get some more. I have
haul'd it to Santa Cruz. Mr McK.[2] promised to call for it, having some
other business there. We have look'd for him over a week. He will stay
here prehaps a week. So you will have it soon. Theres 1000 ft of 2 1/2
inch, 12 inch & over wide (mark'd as 12 inch). The Sawyers told me if
they cut it 6 inch wide it would be apt to split, while it was green. There
is 50 plank, 18 & 24 ft—46 made the 1000, a few of them being a little
rotten (tho' not to hurt). I made up the 50 plank also 4 pr 24 ft 6 by 6,
8 pr 12 ft 7 by 7, & 4 pr 16 ft 7 by 7. I took the latter because they had
a log 16 ft. handy—& 3000 ft 1 inch. When the Don Q[3] arrives here
I will put on board the rafters & more 1 inch lumber. The Pot was high

---

[1] Jacob P. Leese. Bancroft, IV, 710-711.

[2] James McKinley. Bancroft, IV, 725.

[3] *Don Quixote*, American bark, John Meek, master, and William S. Hinckley, supercargo, traded to California from Honolulu in 1833-34 and subsequently.

enough, I know. But had often been offer'd 120$ but keep it to use myself. This Summer concluded not to use it, get $120 if possible for it. If not, any thing above $100—as its down there I need not keep it on hand. Our townsman Mr Hall J. Kelly[4] is yet here. He says you treated him like a brute. (N.B. you did not flatter him & give him a few dolls. I expect). He is now living with me, expects to start next week. 10 sailors agreed to go with him, but all back out. Capt Young[5] has now promised to go. If he should never be king of the Oregon, I think he may be call'd King of Beggers. I sett him down as the greatest Bore I ever knew. I shall be happy to see him start. I think his book will combined the beauties of Mrs Royal[6] & John Bull in America.[7] Did you ever reed the two last?

Yours in hast
T.O. Larkin

NB I have this week taken half of the house of Mrs Hartnell.[8] Having got my business on the Salines something to my liking shall now live at town.   L.

[Larkin to Stearns, S. Coll.]

Monterrey Augt 9, 1834

Mr Abel Stearns

By Capt Meek[9] I ship 4 joice [joists] 24 ft—8 joice 12 ft. 7 by 7— 4 do 16-ft 7-by-7—and a 1000 ft of 2 1/2 inch plank. My reasons for sending it 12 inch wide see my last. As a few of the plank were defective tho' not to hurt, I tho' [sic] in a few. There is 50 in all. I understand two where left at Santa Cruz also 3 m. 5 inch boards, which they

---

4 Hall J. Kelley, the first "Oregon Booster." Bancroft, IV, 697.

5 Ewing Young, captain of trappers. Came to California in 1830. Went to Oregon in 1834 and returned in 1837. Died in Oregon, 1841. Bancroft, V, 782-783.

6 Mrs. Anne Newport Royall, American traveler and author (1769-1854). Wrote *The Black Book; or, a Continuation of Travels in the United States, Mrs. Royall's Pennsylvania, Mrs. Royall's Southern Tour*, etc.

7 James K. Paulding, *John Bull in America; or, the New Munchausen* (New York, 1825), satirizes British travelers in the United States and their books.

8 Mrs. William E. P. Hartnell was María Teresa, daughter of Don José de la Guerra y Noriega. For an account of the Hartnells see Bancroft, III, 777-778; also Susanna Bryant Dakin, *The Lives of William Hartnell* (Stanford, 1949).

9 John Meek. Bancroft, IV, 736.

could not take nor will they take any here. Mr Shaw[10] has promised to that [sic] them. I have ready the rafters, the 2 inch plank 18 ft. Some 1 inch, 4 or 5 m and some doors. Will attend to them, untill they are all shipt.

Yours &c
T. O. Larkin

Capt Young started from the Salines farm, yesterday for the Oregon—expects to return next spring. He takes our Friend Kelly. Thanks be given for his departure.

[*Added in Stearns's handwriting:* Answered 29th Agt.]

[Larkin to Stearns, S. Coll.]

Mont. Aug 10 1834

Mr. Capt. Meek—I shipt some thick stuff. By Capt Hinkley[11]—I send 400 ft. 2 in. stuff & 60 Rafters. They are the size you wrote for—tho' to me they appear short.

I am sorry I have not been able to ship any 1 inch Lumber. The 3 m. I put at Santa Cruz Capt M. could not take it—and Capt Wilson[12] only to Santa B.

Owing to such a stirr among the Sawyers to go with Kelly, there has been but little work. Among them they owe me several ml. & have run off owing me 5 m. I have much Lumber at Santa Cruz. When it can be shipt dont know. Will send Joice & Lumber every chance. Mr Spear[13] ships plenty of Flour by the Don Q.

I think Mr Peck will take some Lumber from the Auctosh[14] in Sept.

Yrs in hast
T. O. Larkin

[*Added in Stearns's handwriting:* Answered Agt. 29th]

---

[10] Thomas Shaw. Bancroft, V, 718.

[11] William Sturgis Hinckley. Native of Massachusetts. Came to California in 1830. Became a Mexican citizen and was alcalde of Yerba Buena in 1844 and captain of the port there, 1845-46. Died in June 1846 at the age of 39. Bancroft, III, 785-786.

[12] John Wilson, Scottish shipmaster and trader. Arrived in California in 1826. Bancroft, V, 777.

[13] Nathan Spear. Bancroft, V, 730.

[14] A place on or near the coast between Santa Cruz and Monterey. Most probably a corruption of "Aptos."

[Larkin to Stearns, S. Coll.]

Mont Dec[r] 3[d] 1834

Mr Abel Stearns
Dr Sr

Yours of Sept. has been rec'd. I wish that Rafter affair could be investigated so that I could chg[e] the amt to some one. Mr Temple[15] a year back wrote he would pay half loss but I do not wish to chg[e] it to him if possible. The lesser sum I named in my last was right. I know now I came to name the larger.

Please ask Mr Rhea[16] to show you my letter I send with this. The 2 1/2 inch stuff I acknowedge was high, partly owing to be sawed to order, but chiefly to Capt Hinkley's pay 125$ for 6 m. at the time 55$ is the market price for one inch.

If possible I will not draw for all that amt. at present. Mr Hays[17] is now waiting—for iron frows, the smith being drunk. I have agreed to find him in tools & a man & wood—totaly to make 64 000 m, I taking half. They are to be made at Armisti's[18] red woods. The ground is to wet in the winter at the Auctosh. I own some trees at Armisti. He *now* refuses to sell at 10$ pr tree. I would not recommend you to have them haul'd to the Auctosh unless you are very sure of a Vessels going there. To Mont. I can have them haul'd at 3$ per m. To the former place it would cost about 1$. To M. is the surest if you want them next summer. If you can sell mine at 11$ for m. on this beach, or 9$ at the Auctosh—sell them, and I will ship them providing nothing prevents which they present state of affairs here do not warrant. I will endeavour to forward Mr H.[19] as far as possible. Times are giting too warm our way, altho', in all that [is] said and done, you know much must be allowed for bad interpretation.

---

15 John Temple. Native of Massachusetts. Came to California in 1827 from Honolulu in the *Waverly.* Engaged in trade at Los Angeles. Died in San Francisco, 1866. Bancroft, V, 745.

16 John Rhea, American trapper from New Mexico. Came to California in 1831. Kept a saloon in Los Angeles. Bancroft, V, 692-693.

17 Elias Hayes, American at Monterey, 1833-36. Bancroft, III, 780.

18 José Amestí, Mexican resident and trader in Monterey (Bancroft, II, 696). The Amestí adobe (shown in the title-page view) still stands on Polk Street.

19 Presumably Elias Hayes.

Mr T. G. Tombuson[20] some time back open'd a small grog shop on nothing. By much trouble & perseverrence he in 5 or 6 months accumulated as many hundred dolls. He at first allowed a very bad set to gather round near all night to gamble. He was in time fined 5$., and told for the second offence should be fined double, for the third ship'd. One sunday morn. the Alcalde call'd on him, and orderd him to prison, & as he says A.G.T. giving no reasons. There they keep him 24 hours. Some time back'd a whaler sail'd after losing some men. In 3 or 4 days he put back & brot a shore a paper, perporting to be signed by some of crew, saying a certain sailor living a shore had tried to induced some of his men to leave, & offered them 14$ per mo. On the strenght of this paper, he was found, pressd on board a Mexican Vessel & rec'd several days. He prehaps deserved it, but one might suppose this paper should be proved. 3d last week a Boy came to me, wishing me to hire him. I ask'd him if he had a passport. Said no. I told him to go to Geo. Allen,[21] have his declaration made out saying he came a shore without permit, & if he could then get a passport I would hire him, but not before—'twas done. The Alcalde being absent, the 2d sign it. Unknowned be known to me, Allen in writing the passport, named him as my servant—the Boy I had never before seen. I then hired him—after the 2 A. said he was free to go to work. That day the Boy was put on board the Frigate—next day Mr 2d ask'd me to go with him to Madirin's[22] (Capt of the Port). There he show'd me a paper, left a shore it appears by the Boy Capt, saying he had left his ship & owed 50 or 60$, and the Gen's orders were that I must pay the amt. I told him the Gen had been misinformd and wish'd to go and see him. He said that was not his business, and I must pay it, & I *should not* call on the Gen. untill I had. I offer'd Security—but No. I was told to go home & get the cash, and if I call'd on the Gen. in going home, he would *imprison* me, even if I said one word to him. In going home, I met Mr Hartnell. He wish'd to go to the Gen., but as this 2d Alcalde was there as

---

[20] Presumably Ambrose G. (or Thomas L.) Tomlinson or Thomason, known also as "Tom the Trapper," from New Mexico, who settled in California in 1832. Bancroft, V, 749.

[21] George Allen. Irish or British. Came to California in 1822. Kept a shop or inn at Monterey and was also in government employ as justice of the peace, etc. Was employed as consular clerk by Larkin, 1845-46. Died at Monterey, 1847. Bancroft, II, 690-691.

[22] Probably Bonifacio Madariaga, Mexican official at Monterey, 1830-42. Bancroft, IV, 727.

first, I objected. Don J. J. Gomez[23] told me not to pay it first, but see the Gen. As my Wife had been inform'd of it and was very uneasy, I pd it into the Capt of the port hands for the present & I suppose for ever. I then call'd on the Gen[l] & told him my story. He said he had been told quite different & that I had hired the boy knowing him to be with out passports &c, but if my story was true, it should be pd back. Since then I have gone from him to [the] Capt. of the P. & Vice Versa, but they have not time to see to it—what will you give me for the money.—4[d] Within the last month, the Alcalde, Dñ Manuel, has been calling in all Foreigners to make out their Declaration—where they came from & how they came, giving each on his signing the D. a passport, binding him to present himself every month. The Gen[l] has said, in fact told John & I, yesterday, that he was determined to send every Foreigner out of the Country, that had not a Passport from the particular State he came from. He was sorry &c. but orders had been rec'd to that effect. John ask'd him if a passport from Mr Jones[24] would not do. No. It might do from the Consul in C. if there was one. He askd if passports brot here by hunting Capt. did not protect the men. No. Each man must have one. Now there may be some mistake here, but so we this week understand it. I have one passport from Gov Lincoln of Mass—but should not like to be left alone here. If law here, law with you. There is certainly some F—in C. that should be sent out, tho' I think some there is—who are a benifit to the place. Let what will happen I hope they wont call on me for any more 50$. I was robb'd last month of 300$ —and cant stand too many such hauls. There is one sailor here to whom Spence[25] is rather partial. I lately told him up for stealing a horse of mine—and impriso[ned] him & fined him. I understand that Spence told the 2[d] Alcalde & the Capt of the P. for this I ought to suffer & be compell'd to pay this 50$. These Scotch.

In relately any thing in this, give it on hear say. I tell you (excepting the 50$ scrape that I know happend), these things as they tell to me— I think times are gitting tough—but every thing one hears may not

---

23 José Joaquín Gómez, Mexican trader and official who came to California in 1830. Longtime friend of Larkin, who was captured at Gómez' ranch in 1846 during the Mexican War. Bancroft, III, 758-759.

24 John Coffin Jones, Jr., of Boston, a merchant and U.S. consul at Honolulu from 1830, who settled in Santa Barbara in 1841. Bancroft, IV, 694-695.

25 David Spence. Native of Scotland. Came to California from Peru in 1824. Alcalde of Monterey in 1835 and holder of many offices under the Mexican and U.S. governments there. Died in 1875. Bancroft, V, 730-731.

happen. My case I call a hard one. Giving security was denied. Weather that paper was a forgery—or weather the Capt was a lyar, I nor they do not know.

Yours

T. O. Larkin

[Larkin to Stearns, S. Coll.]

Mont Nov 9, 1836

Mr Abel Stearns
Sir

Yours of Aug was rec'd this week. When I gave or sign'd the papers for H— I told him I had forgot all the curcumstances—and good [sic] sign nothing certain. And now forget what I gave him. He told me when he return'd he was to recover all. Mr Garner[26] goes your way, & you can talk with him. Altho' the shingles where not rec'd [in] time, as I could not leave. I think they were done [MS torn] ways told H. to be satisfied with his pay, and let [MS torn] the forfiets. But he goes for all he says. If I could not obtain my Bond with Myers, I do not see how he can with you.

By Garner you will hear of the Revolution this way. There is about 30 Foreigners under pay at the gaurd house. The Gen, Munez, District judge, & some others are sent off. Now on board. More are to be sent they say. I presume you will see their printed paper. I send you one. This will for a long time cause unsettled times in C. We must however get along as we can. The flag is to be six stripes & one Star, they say. It has broke up all work here for the present. I wish it was ended, for times to go Smooth again.

Yours in much hast

T. O. Larkin

---

26 William Robert Garner. Native of London, deserter from an English whaler at Santa Barbara ca. 1826. Engaged in lumber business at Monterey. Killed by Indians in 1849 after going to the mines. Bancroft, III, 754.

[Larkin to Stearns, S. Coll.]

Monterey Dec 8 1842

Mr Abel Stearns
Sir

Hearing two or three times, that as the General[27] is waiting for the Com[28] at San Pedro, you all are continually on the look out for him, I take an opportunity that offers to give you some information on the Subject.

Com Jones (I believe) informed the Gen. that he would meet him at San Pedro, about the 15 of Nov. At that time and to this day he is waiting for the Ship of war Dale, that was sent into Panama for the latest U.S. news. She has not yet arrived—and the Com. does not like to leave here untill she does arrive. About two weeks back I told him that General Michterneno [Micheltorena] was waiting for his appearance, and it would be well to inform him why he could [not] leave here. It was that day reported that a mail was then making up for the Pueblo, as one had just come in from Sonoma. The Com[r] sat down at my table and wrote to the Gen. This was given to the Authorities here. Since then the letter and I believe the mail was given to Mr W[m] D. Howard[29] who was hunting up Horses to go down. The Jos. Peabody then came in, and the Captain said he would sail the next day or the day after. Mr H. then went on board her, where he is still wind bound. He has now saild for Santa Barbara [*altered from* He will sail for Santa Barbara I suppose today].

The letter of the Com. you see has for over 2 weeks been detaind by one cause or other as the Gov. does not live here. Prehaps the mails are less certain to go & come to M. Its a pity that the Gen. should be detained. I think he's much wanted here. Report speaks well of him. His letter to the Com. shows him to be one well acquanted with the ways of the world—the sooner he appears in Mont—I think the better for all here. I hope he will not wait for the Com. The Dale ought to have arrived 30 days ago, yet may have Sunk, and never arrive.

---

[27] Manuel Micheltorena, governor and commanding general of California, 1842-45. Bancroft, IV, 740.

[28] Commodore Thomas Ap Catesby Jones (1790-1858). *Dictionary of American Biography*, X, 201.

[29] William Davis Merry Howard. Native of Boston. Came to California in 1839. Close business associate of Larkin for many years. Died in 1856. Bancroft, III, 788-789.

I suppose you hear many reports of affairs here, and of the Gov. He is yet at his Rancho, and I suppose means to remain there. The times are bad here, all is at a stand. The arrival of the Gen. in M. will alter this. They have a large house under hire for him.

Yours, &c

Thomas O. Larkin

NB. We have no expectation of any new Vessels [MS torn] much duties at present the George & He [torn] to take the place of the Corsair, will be [torn] next month. No Cargo, coming for the Corsa[ir] [torn] (no hides) there is no Vessel in Oahu. up [torn] Should Mr Thompson[30] go down & bring cargo—I suppose he will have the duties in his own hands—as debts we are over run with goods, and no soon sale. My sales have been double and collections but 1/3, for 1842—in Comparison to 1841.

Yours &c

T. O. L.

[Larkin to Stearns, S. Coll.]

Monterey Apr. 18. 1843

Mr Abel Stearns

I forward a letter for Dn Luis Vignes[31] from Parrott & Co, one letter for Dn M. Pedronera,[32] and three for Capt. Fitch[33] to your care.

The Cyane arrived here last week from Mazatlan (28 days). The English have faught much in China, and have succeeded in making a treaty. The chinese open five Ports to trade, allow Consuls in each, grant forever an Island to the Queen, paid 6 000 000 at the time, and 15 more within 2 or 4 years, the English holding some Ports as security. The Tartar Gen, on finding himself beat, placed himself in a chair in his own house, & order'd his servants to fire the building, and burnt up in

---

30 Joseph P. Thompson. Native of Massachusetts. Came to California probably in 1839-40 as supercargo in ship *Joseph Peabody*. Bancroft, V, 747.

31 Jean Louis Vignes, French cooper and distiller who came to California from Honolulu on the *Louisa* in 1831. Died in Los Angeles in 1862. Bancroft, V, 762-763.

32 Miguel Pedrorena, Spanish supercargo of the brigs *Delmira* and *Juan José*, 1837-40. Settled in California. Member of Constitutional Convention of 1849. Died in 1850. Bancroft, IV, 770.

33 Henry Delano Fitch. Native of New Bedford, Mass. Came to California in 1826. Master of the *Leonor*, 1830-31. Died in San Diego, 1849. Bancroft, III, 739-740.

the chair. Many of the Natives destrowed their Families and themselfs. Some wells were found with the whole family in it. By this treaty, a new and great trade has opened in china to English goods. The Yankees will of course see to it, as far as their Interest is concerned. Queen V. and the great cousin of the moon will soon have Ministers at each other courts, I suppose. The latter would not sign the treaty first. He said, Ladies first. The English have also gained in their E. I. possesions, and retaking their Officers and Wifes back again from the Natives. The Londoners & other where greatly rejoicing on receiving the two Treaties. All London was in a Smoke.

The Cyane brought only one letter for General Mitchetoneno [Micheltorena]. I think it was wrote in Mazatlan. I gave it to the Captain of the Port, so I suppose the Gen. has it. The drafts taken down by the Frenchman and John C. Jones, Esq from Gen M. on the Custom House at Mazatlan, I understand were not paid and that the Holders had no prospects of payment. Mr Jones left in three days. I suppose that he, Thompson & Paty[34] will be here in 15 days. I have N.Y. papers 80 days old, up to last of January. They contain Mexican news of December. They say that Santa Anna discharged the Congress, by request of some of the Juntas of the States, which request he obtained to sent [serve] his own views. The Gov't. has now ordered a new Congress of 40 men who are to make a new constitution, which must be approved of by the President and his Ministers before it becomes law. Gen. Santa Anna is President without restriction. For six months in Dec he was residing on his Estate near Vera Cruz. His Steamers & Brigs had taken Troops to Campeachy, and was there fighting. After taking that place 'twas supposed they would go to Texas. The English Post Captain, and other English officers on board the great Steamer, had been recalled to London. Every thing in the Republic was quite. Congress, on breaking up, had a little to say against it. 'Twas only in words however. The Army was strong. Affairs in Texas was quite, their Army small, their Navy about to be disbanded. I believe they were taking some towns on the Rio Grande. I think a town called Loredo and some places near it, but I dont know. Mexico had a new Taraff go into force 25 of last January. Coloured Cotten 13 cents, plain do 15 cts. and some pr centage on that. Supposed about 3/4 higher than the Taraff of 1842. I should think that would prevent Mantas coming to California. So we have no grain, no

---

34 John Paty. Native of Massachusetts and merchant at Honolulu from 1833. First came to California in 1837. Master of the *Don Quixote*, 1838-48. Died in Honolulu, 1868. Bancroft, IV, 769.

killing of cattle. Drafts on Mazatlan below par, and but few duties coming in for this 1843.

Captain Stribling[35] informed me that he could hear of no Vessel bound to C. from Mazatlan. I suppose that the Gen. waits for one before he marches for this place, if he is to come. Its a pity he did not at once, and see the place, and then things would not remain in so great and uncertainity. I think his presence is desired here.

The Mexican papers were full of Com. Jones' affair. One said that thanks to Santa Anna & Torriel, the Com found California in such a high state of defence, he back[ed] out, and made the best excuse he could. I believe that Gen M. acct. was also published. How they suppose he is to protect the country without funds is hard to say. I believe there is no chance of a dollar being sent to him, or any of his Drafts excepted. The N.O. & N. York papers have a little to say about the Comodore. A call in Congress, on the President Tyler, was made for information on the subject, which information was not then given. I suppose the Com. will be recalled, and thats all as far as hes concerned. If Mexico demands damages I suppose Congress will allow it, if given credet in the old acct. Minister Thompson has been ordered to make a formal demand on Mexico for a payment of the debts admitted, and Settlement for the ballance. I think the former is 2 1/2 000 000, the latter 8 000 000. Its some time since I saw the acct. The house of Senate has passed an act, to take possesion of the Origon, giving to each Settler who will cultivate five years 640 acres, his Wife 320, each child 120 —do— I suppose they will soon make a settlement of that country. The line is nigher Yerba Buena than Monterey is to Santa Barbara. What comes next time will come.

As I am not a Correspondent of yours, you will think I have wrote rather a long letter. As there appeared some news of importance I wished my different acquantance your way might have the news. If Mr Howard is in San Diego, I wish you would Send this letter to him, therby save me the writing of a nother.

Yours &c.

Thomas O. Larkin

I rec'd your letter.

[*Written across lower right bottom of letter in a different handwriting (probably not Abel Stearns's):* Thomas O. Larkin Carta Abril 18, 1843. Tells of the result of the English Chinese opium war and much gossip.]

---

35 C. K. Stribling, captain of U.S.S. *Peacock*, 1836, and commander of U.S.S. *Cyane*, 1842-43 and 1845. Bancroft, V, 737.

II. Trader *cum* Consul

March - August 1845

THOMAS LARKIN received his letter of appointment as United States consul in California on April 2, 1844, and immediately handed over the bulk of his business responsibilities to Talbot H. Green, who had been his clerk and now became his partner. Though he could now devote a considerable proportion of his time to his consular functions, his letters remain full of matters concerning trade, his debts and loans, and his many other activities. Hardly a letter refers to official business exclusively. It must be remembered, of course, that Larkin now began (and continued until 1848) his series of reports and dispatches to the State Department, first collected by Bancroft in "Documents for the History of California" and now in process of publication in *The Larkin Papers*. The letters here printed present more frankly Larkin's private thoughts, anxieties, and frustrations than does his official correspondence, and they take the reader more behind the scenes of Larkin's already developing project to interest the United States in the acquisition of California and to interest the Californians in having their territory acquired by the United States.

Larkin's appointment came too late for it to be possible for him to influence in any material way, either by his dispatches to the State Department or by his articles sent to the editors of eastern newspapers, the expansionist sentiment of the Democratic party in the election campaign of 1844. But California was soon to take its place alongside Texas and Oregon as a primary objective of United States government policy, though the Whig administration of Tyler had paid little attention to the pleas of Waddy Thompson (American minister to Mexico) that the acquisition of California was worth any sacrifice. Larkin—as his dispatches began to be read in Washington and his articles to be printed in the East—by the autumn of 1845 started to play a major part in publicizing California and making it as much coveted as Oregon and Texas. Not content with his own efforts, he sent the two very persuasive letters to Dr. John Marsh (a man whom in fact he disliked), urging Marsh to write everything he could "in favor" of California and "I will have it published in the N.Y. papers." Marsh, after some delay, did even better than this and wrote directly to Senator Lewis Cass of Michigan, who sent his long, California-boosting letter to the press, where it was widely reprinted.

The revolution that deposed and sent into exile the new governor of Alta California, General Micheltorena, split the American and European community into two factions. Sutter and (at first) Marsh supported the general, but Stearns and many others preferred Alvarado, José Castro, and Pío Pico, his opponents. Larkin, lacking information on the progress of the movement (as his letter to Marsh of March 18, 1845, clearly indicates), tried to remain neutral, though he had lent support and money to Micheltorena before the outbreak and stood to lose much by his removal. When Micheltorena was exiled, Larkin took his losses (which Stearns told him were his own fault) philosophically and sought to establish good relations with the new regime. Nevertheless, Larkin was discriminated against by having the payment of government debts to him withheld. His consular position prevented him from protesting (in public at least) as vigorously as he would have wished.

That rumors were already flying concerning a change of sovereignty in Alta California is indicated by David Spence's letter to Leidesdorff and Thomas Jefferson Farnham's letter to Marsh in 1845. In the latter letter the idea of a "Republic of California" is broached by the enthusiastic author of *Travels in the Great Western Prairies* and *Life and Adventures in California*.

[Larkin to Stearns, S. Coll.]

Monterey March 4, 1845

Mr Abel Stearns
Dear Sir—

Unexpected to me Gov. Pico has forwarded his orders to Don Pablo, as administrador not to pay any Government debts, untill the accounts of the Aduana are attended to. I have several thousand Dollars in

Drafts on this Aduana, drawn by General Micheltorena, and accepted by the Adm^r payable from the 1, 2, & 3^d Vessels entering and paying over 10000$ each, the first Vessel being 4250$ as due me.

You are aware that there are many with high expectations from the new Vessels. By the change of affairs in this country, the new Govenor may be some time in regulating the payment of the old Gov. debts, altho' he has expressed a wish to settle them soon as possible. In the mean time, the duties by different orders on the new Supercargoes, by Srs Castro or others, may be absolved while the orders are making out to pay me and a large entry of 10,000$ does not happen every month. The Comisaria is also owing me about 2000$. Exclusive of this I have a Government a/c. to settle with the General on his arrival.

My object in writing to you is to request you will call on the Gov. and obtain an order for me on the Administrador that I may have orders given to me on the new Vessels as they enter, first, second & third, to pay the respective sums as first agreed on, and recorded in the Custom House Books. Even when these orders are accepted by the Supercargoes they have 4, 6 and 9 months time to pay the cash & Hides. You may think I have large sums against the General. I have. He even owes me for near 2000 silver dollars lent him in *1843*. My Mazatlan debts where 12,000$ besides the funds I carried there. All these goods and [sic] gone, and I owe near 3000$ in Cash & bearing interest, in Monterey, by reason of my selling so much and lending so much Cash to the General during 43 & 44.

Should the Spring Vessels enter and get out of there duties, I not paid, I must wait untill /46. Even now I am out of goods and my trade stopt for want of funds.

It is my intention to write to the new Gov. on this subject, but may not have time to send it translated. I must therefore depend on your assistance with the expectations of hearing from you by return Mail.

Captain Vincent[1] was diing at Mr Spear' house last week of the consumption. Why Mr Park[2] winters it there don't know.

When Gen M. left here I think he had many Friends. By his astonishing delay they found the country would have no peace by his exer-

---

[1] If the reference is to George W. Vincent, he did not in fact die until 1851, in the great San Francisco fire of that year. A native of Massachusetts, he came first to California in 1826 and from 1844 to 1846 commanded the ship *Sterling*. Bancroft, V, 763.

[2] Thomas B. Park. Native of Massachusetts. First came to California in 1826 as supercargo of the *Harbinger*. Acted as supercargo of the *Sterling*, 1844-46. Died in Santa Barbara about 1850. Bancroft, IV, 767.

tions. They therefore by degrees fell off. By the time we heard of the final result (excepting 4/5 of the Mexicans in M.) most of the People here were prepared to hope it would so prove.

I am decidely a Government Upholder, while the same Govt can be worthy of any confidence. To the last minute I suppled Gen M, & I will see him to his house and shud [?] see him on board, the same now as if he was the Conquerer. As the Country is now under new Rulers, when they become settled, I shall disapprove of a Revolution as much as I did three months back, and will assist a new Gov. the same as I did the old one.

I am very sorry a single Foreigner took up arms in the late affair. Sutter, to do away the ideom [odium?] on him and his Neighbors, as thro' on him in Mexico, will do away much disconfidence there. So far so good. Otherwise it was bad. Those who took up arms against the established Gov't done worse in my opinion. They and their property, for an age, may suffer for it, by some iron handed Mexican Gen.

I consider this country in a very unsettled state. If Mexico would give the command to the sons of the country, and these sons would not divide the power, quarrel for the power and the loaves & fishes, we may live happy. There is no use in saying that Mexico can not or will not send more soldiers here. Soldier[s] can be had in the Republic, by scouring the streets, and if she does send, they will be sent away. Mexico can at intervals do as she pleases with C. and each Revolution here hurt the country, destroys the animals [?] & demoralizes the people. I therefore hope the country may by the Prisedent be permited to remain under the Rulers new in office, and these Rulers may bring forward the People, and these recourses.

I am

Yours &c

Thomas O. Larkin

My respects to Mrs Stearns
and her sister Miss Isadora.[3]

---

[3] Mrs. Stearns was Arcadia, daughter of Juan Bandini, and her sister Isidora (later Mrs. Cave J. Couts) is presumably the one referred to here by Larkin. Their mother was Dolores, daughter of José M. Estudillo.

[*Larkin to Marsh, Ma. Coll. CSL*]

Monterey, March 18, 1845.

Dr. John Marsh—
Sir:

From every person who I speak to respecting the journey of General to the south I obtain a different statement, as you can well described the journey being present with your ears and eyes open (which has been the case with every one) I ask from you a long discription of your trip, and such views and opinions as you can give me on the present state of affairs.

I believe not a single Foreigner who joined the party has passed through M[onterey]., their accounts I therefore receive second hand and am like to do so for a time.

The General nor Sr Castro has yet arrived. We have no direct news of their movements this the 25 of February. I believe they are entering the Tasso in San Diego. If the Farmers near Mont. fought for gain, they may find an Irish one, unless Don Jose helps matters.

Yours &c
Thomas O. Larkin

[*Larkin to Stearns, S. Coll.*]

Monterey May 21 1845

Mr. Abel Stearns
Sir—

Your favor for Mr Howard I have rec'd (dated 13th).[4]

I had none, nor have I any fear but the new Governor has a proper disposition towards paying the debts of Gen. M. I do not like the idea of there laughing at the protest, as I should make it again, if again so situatted.

You appear supprised that the Merchants of this place trusted M. so much. I think those of *Mont.* amounted to about 12000$ most of which were in my name. I understand that the merchants of the Pueblo trusted the new Gov't nearly that sum in as many weeks—the supprise should not therefore be so great. Avarice I presume guided us all.

---

4 See Hammond, III, 184-185, for Stearns's letter of May 13, 1845.

My debts against the *Government* are large, but not against Gen. Micheltorena. As there is no necessity of entering into an Explanation, you may take my word as I write it.

I did "foresee the consequences of trusting Gen. M." *He* as Gov and Gen. owed me 3000 to 4000$ from each of three vessels, and he would have paid me had he remained. And I have faith enough in the new powers to prevent my sending my debts to Mexico as you reccommend. If he owed much it was to others not of Monterey.

You think that I ought to be aware that a Govt debt is not good unless under the knowledge and authority of Congress. So may have read the law in some past day. But *now* I am aware that the Com^t Gen alone has authority with the Commissario respecting the funds. That no Governor has anything to do with these, yet I thought it best to write to his Excellency on the Subject, because he forbid the Administardor to pay debts for the present. If you think this may not be so, I can with ease show you the law to this effect.

In final I am perfectly convinced that the Gov. Com^t Gen. & adm^r will be willing to pay when they have the ability. If there is during 1845, the means, I am confident of the will.

By Capt Vioget[5] I sent you some Newspapers. I take many from home, and can always spare you some if you wish it.

The California has been here a week. Her Cargo cost in B.[6] about 17000$. Capt Stephen Smith[7] comes via Mazatlan. Has no vessel. Has a little mill work & furniture on board. Its uncertain about any other vessel from B. In Decr there was none up for C. Mr Howard came to day. The *officers* of the Custom house will have coming to them half of the California duties.

Yours in hast
Larkin

---

[5] Jean Jacques Vioget, Swiss sailor and surveyor. Arrived in California in 1837. Bancroft, V, 764.

[6] Boston.

[7] Stephen Smith. Native of Maryland. Arrived in California in 1841, probably on the *Corsair*. ". . . he later told Lieut Sherman that he came to Cal. on the assurance of [Daniel] Webster that the U.S. would surely have the country. . . ." Bancroft, V, 724.

[Spence to Leidesdorff, LE 51]

Monterey 14th June 1845

Dear Sir:

I enclose you Mr. Howards Pagare for $455.0—I could not get him to accept it for less time. The other due bills of the Generals none has been paid.

Don Manuel Diaz arrived yesterday by land from Sta Barba. He frighted the Julia, landed there and dispatched her for this port. We expect her every day. She, I believe, is to go to San Franco and then return to San Blas for Mr. Dalton.[8]

Otro Cosa There is two thousand Mexican troops all ready waiting in Acapulco for vessels to come on to California. The English minister has some hand in this affair as they are to be paid by two English compys in Mexico. We may expect them in one or two months. This is no story. You can rely upon it as a truth.

The war is all settled. Texas is accknowledged by the Mexicans as and Independent state, guaranteed by the English and French that the Yankes will never never take it in to the Union.

Yours very truly
D. Spence

[Farnham to Marsh, Ma. Coll. CSL]

New York,
90 Wall Street
July 6, 1845

Doctor Marsh,

My dear freind, I have thought of you almost daily since I left you at Monterey, & have strongly desired to write you; but feared that by so doing I should subject you again to the tyrranical suspicions of the Spaniards; for I can write to no person in California, without expressing the strongest desire of my heart, to wit, that the "Republic of California" should arise—exist—& shed the blessings of Freedom over that delightful land.

---

[8] Henry Dalton, English trader from Lima. Came to California in 1843. Bancroft, II, 773-774.

Will you pardon me for a suggestion—Neither Europe or the States are yet prepared for that event. The excitement consequent on the admission of Texas into the Union must have time to abate. The winter of 46 will do. Next year will see me & my family, God willing, at your house. From 10 to 20 thousand emigrants will enter California next summer. There will then be population enough to *authorise* the step; & we shall have force enough for any contingency.

Excuse the haste with which I write. And believe me your *fellow citizen of California* & your sincere friend.

Thomas J. Farnham

Doctor Marsh
San Francisco
U California

[Larkin to Marsh, Ma. Coll. CSL]

Monterey, July 8, 1845

Mr. John Marsh
Sir

Within an hour I have rec'd yours of yesterday.[9] I can hardly inform who or what is coming to Monterey, rather to California, nor when. Reports have arrived here that 1800 Troops are to be dispatched to this country from Acupulco, that Consul Parrott of Mazatlan had 70,000$ to fit out the expedition and 2 or 3 English Houses are responsible for the pay of these Troops for 18 months, and that by the desire or instigation of Eng. M. is sending them on. Now Mr. Parrott informs me that he had no funds for this purpose, that the Catilina was waiting in A., the German ship Occean in Mazt. Gov't wished Mr. P. to advance funds, and be security for the O. charter, which he refused. A mail had been sent to the Capital on the subject & would return 8 days after Mr P. left. He thinks 700 Soldiers will come on, under Gen Inestro, a Mexican educated in the famous Paris School, and the money he will bring and afterwards rec'd from M. will be on a par of what always been in such cases.

---

9 Marsh's letter of July 7, 1845, from San Jose was printed by Hammond, III, 259-260. This reply by Larkin of July 8 was printed in part by George D. Lyman in his *John Marsh, Pioneer* (New York, 1930), pp. 268-269, but less than half of the letter is quoted by Lyman and that in an edited form which omits Larkin's criticism of Marsh for his "apathy and idleness" and for appearing "one the most behind, for your talant" in California.

sario jointly and I will present one, two, or all according to the quantity of goods in Government hands at the time.

Should this business be instrusted to me, I shall attend to it as it should be attended to, and charge the usual commissions for my trouble, and warrent that it shall prove satisfactory to all of you whom it may concern.

Should this offer be accepted an express should be forwarded immediately, and I should be instructed to take such cash and goods as I can get, and give such prices as I may think just to all parties, to bring into effect the entry. Should the express be delayed, the Vessel may go away, as Sen Abrego[11] is paid to take in charge so many goods at a time.

On my receiving any goods I should send you an express at once, and hold myself ready to receive the Gov.' orders from 1$ each to 10,000$. You may think this a wild speculation, but if you was here you would advise Gov. Pico to embrace it.

I am &c Yours
Thomas O. Larkin

[Larkin to Stearns, S. Coll.]

Monterey July 20 1845

Mr. Abel Stearns
Sir—

Your favor of—1—have rec'd. Please send the Alcahol soon as may be ready.

I am aware that it would be well if the Northern Deputies would attend the sessions, as you observe, but they may think like many more that those of the South are trying to reverse the state of affairs by removal of the Capital, Custom House, Etc. Etc., in which case they can do alone as well as in company of those from the North, the latter being to few to be heard at the Vote. Of course parties, both N & S, mean to have the seat of Government where it best pleases themselfs, and the trade & commerce of the country must remain fluctuating during the uncertainty. Should those below succeed, some 10 or 15 years hence it will be so understood and conformed to. During this time affairs will be in a state [of] effervescence, and those not afraid of troubled waters will sail on the sufface and profit accordingly. It mat-

---

11 José Ábrego, *subcomisario* and treasurer in charge of the territorial finances of Alta California, 1839-46. Bancroft, II, 686.

ters not to me how things go or have their being. I can keep pace with the people and curcumstances around me.

You may have heard that for two or three years I have wished to bring about an araingment to have Vessels whose cargoes were put up for other ports enter at this place on some certain terms, pay their duties in cash, and carry from this coast *all* their cargo, by which act some 50. to 100 000$ in cash might reach C. and the other Vessels receive no injury. Last year 10 000$ was to have been put on board the Sch^r C[alifornia]. to enter into this business, but the shipment was prevented by the Sch^r being hurried off with the mail. This month an opportunity was again offered, but tho' the peculiar feelings of one in the C[ustom]. H[ouse]. no cash arraingment was held out to the vessel. But an offer was made by those in office to enter in full supposed duties 38 or 40000$, paying 4000$ in cash, the ballance in goods at such prices as to make it an offer to the Vessel. Sr A.[12] was anxious for a cash contract, Mr. H.[13] willing, but Don P[ablo]. who only have the vessel enter only by law, and then Gov't might take goods at prices as per agreement. As it was supposed dishonest to take 20 or 30000$ for 60000, a way was found to take 60. for 30$ cash versus goods.

Over 30,000$ of Gov't debts have been paid Individuals, besides a large amt. to Gov't. officers. The C. H. officers lost their part of the cash, and they even had to take goods. Sr A. has showed a disposisition [sic] that one could not dream of in Sr Pico, in paying debts to every one without distintion of persons or quality of debts. That shamefull decree (not yet repealed) debaring me from collecting my debts, the oldest due by Gov't, must recoiled on those who advised or gave it, when they know it was a dead letter from its reaching this place and hence forward will continue to be. Orders have been given for thousands of dollars (of the same class of mine) of debts to be paid, yet the order respecting mine is not yet recinded, and had it not been for me, I believe Gen M. & troops could not have gone to sea for want of provissions. I am thus repaid. Since this order has been promulgated in M[onterey]., two of Gov. Pico papers, one as low as 200$, has been hacked about M for sale, particularly, and no purchaser offered himself —But Bah. I began this letter for something else.

Don Pablo goes to your place "he says" to explain the last entry and seak instructions respecting the next one, daily expecting with a cargo worth prehaps in duties 80 to 100 000$. He says the vessel will remain here untill he returns. I know better, or rather in the strict sence of the

---

12 Probably José Ábrego.
13 Probably W. D. M. Howard.

word, the vessel may, not the non entry. That will soon be over, if we can come to terms. As you may as a Merchant & Creditor of Gov't. and as a Friend of those in power, wish to know how the case may be, I wish to explain to you. Mr Parrott for 2 or 3 years has by low health been prevented from living in Maz[atlan]. in the summer. By my advice he agreed to come here last year but went to Mxº. This year he came here, with a cargo for Sitka & a market. It was with the Brig now at ancror and is with the expected vessel, his intention to go to Oahu unless he can arainge here, there to remain untill to Sept., then touch off here. By Oct. the climate will suit him in Maz. and in that month there will be anew tarif, something similar to that of 1842, when it will admit him on better terms. Now it matters not where he lays untill Oct., here or in Oahu. Captain Fisher is engaged at 3000$ if he is wanted but will not go untill Oct. to Mazatlan. Should Mr Parrot not be able to enter this month, he will appear off here in Sept. and then expects to find the new Gen. an acquantance of his. Under him he says he knows how he can enter. Now altho' once a Friend to Gen. M. he is now way from C. and I am as much a Friend of the new powers, and we may not choose to see the new General in possesion of 30 or 40000$ of Mr P. funds to battle the match against the natives of C. Therefore for this reason and to collect the debts againt the present Gov't., we ought to have the entry of this vessel, either on terms all cash or for a little cash & much goods at high prices. Even the latter does not now appear high once [?] the quality is seen. Either way Mr P. will anchor if there is not to many voices in the trade. He says every one appears to be everything as the occation serves, and will not enter where this too much confusion and too many ordering. He is perfectly willing to remain between this place & San Diego untill Oct. or go to Oahu, there sell a little of his cargo and appear of[f] M. in September, enter or not as curcumstances may dictate.——If you would have any debts againt Gov't. collected from this new cargo, or any other person, I will attend to them, but they should be sent up by express.

I am &c
Thomas O. Larkin

[Larkin to Stearns and Temple, S. Coll.]

Monterey July 20, 1845

Mr Abel Stearns & Mr John Temple
Sir

Should you, any other Merchant of your place, or any person under Government pay with their demands collected in this place, I should be happy to attend to the Collection at 5 pr cent on the amt. Collected. I paying Carting & Storage of Monterey.

Having reduced my own Government debts, and having every requisit knowledge respecting the business, I flatter myself I can attend to this business better than any other person, and promise that my own debts shall not interfere in the collecting of others.

You will oblige me by giving this information to each of your Neighbors who may be interested and immediately—as each person must give his instruction, I should advice instructions to be given to take whatever kind of pay may be offered. Should you agree to this plan an express should be sent to me at once. If the Vessel arrives that I expect the amt. however large you may send will make no difference in the collecting for all.

I am &c Yours
Thomas O. Larkin

[Larkin to Stearns, S. Coll.]

Monterey August 18 1845

Mr Abel Stearns
Sir—

Your favor for Don Pablo I have rec'd. I rec'd no orders from the Governor nor any other person to collect debts. I understood that the Gov. said 5 pr ct could not [be] paid for commissions & Storage. Therefore in case of another large entry I shall lose the 5, and he 95 per ct. I could I believe this minute obtain 8000$ of goods for him. Should this prove 7000, 6000 or 3000$ by the time he sees it, he will think the 5 pr ct. well paid had he entered in my arraingments. He had once order' my Gov't debts not to be paid untill farther order. I have rec'd much on the a/c. and when all paid, he may [MS torn] he had the thanks of it.

I shall not ask again. The interest on two papers is more than the Salary of many officers so I can wait. Paid it will be and with the interest. I did not choose to take the whole in goods from the "Matador."

If I had not undertaken the wrecking of the Vessel lately lost,[14] the goods would never have gone to the benifit of the Underwriters or the duties to the Aduana. They would have been carried off. As it is, Carmel is rich. I paid in cash & goods to one poor man near 400$ for his share of silk & muslin. He pic up and died one morning. Hundreds of people kept all. I could get no gaurds from the C.H. or Soldiers for 7 or 8 days. Callico better than ever came here from Boston, has been sold at 2$— Muslin 24 yds. on board worth 24$ the same.

I had all the goods taken from the wreck by Foreigners in Boats that they could get hold off, with irons (the wreck was 15 to 20 ft under water), dried, brot to me and washed. I gave these Men 1/3, I claiming 1/2 of the whole. This gave them 33 in 100—I paying certain expenses & finding food in port & Boats. The half of the goods sold at Auction was 4000$. Mr. Hartnell has Collecter named Messrs Diaz, S. Monrus, Spence, Watson, & Osios to apprise the goods & say the duties. Watson wanted 5 pr ct duties paid. We expected 15. They made it out, to discount on the Tarif. Setled 40. White Manta 50—Prints 60 pr ct. Mr Parrott for some time refused to except the goods but thro them into the C.H. saying some of the articles would hardly paid duties. I had quite a sparring with Mr Spence by letter, he trying to convince me that he never was governd by self interest. Both Alvarado, Parrott & Hartnell objected to the duties as laid down. Mr Parrott at last paid 1600$. He bought 88 ps. of Manta, wide opine 40 yds, which at the price of duties laid by Spence & Co would leave the underwrighter less than 10 per ct of the sales & 5 of the whole amt.

The wreck & Cargo within her, was sold at auction to Dye & 7 others, at 160$ or 170$, who are now are wrecking again. Yesterday they took out 50 ps. creas. & 1 Brass bedstead. Not 8 pr ct of the barels are out. Many are broke up and go[n]e, yet many are still in slight in clear water. There is also in a Bbl with 10 000$, & 45 Brass bedstead, &c.

Yours &c
Thomas O. Larkin

---

14 The *Star of the West* was a schooner of British registry but owned by John Parrott, U.S. consul at Mazatlán. William Atherton was master. She was wrecked off Point Lobos, near Monterey, on July 27, 1845. Her cargo was from Liverpool. See Bancroft, IV, 568, and Parker, "The Wreck of the *Star of the West*," in *Hist. Soc. of So. Calif. Quart.*, XXIII (1941), 24-27, reprinting John A. Swan's MS account of the wreck, written in 1845 (original in the Bancroft Library).

[Larkin to Marsh, Ma. Coll. CSL]

Monterey, August 19, 1845

Dr. John Marsh

Sir—

Your favor for Mr Knight I have rec'd. I can not have any conversation with Sor. Alvarado on the subject you mention.[15] My official station and ideas of Foreigners having anything to do with Government affairs prevents it, most particular the former. There are sufficient in the country both Native & Foreign as it is.

I would again impress on your mind the importance of writing in favor of the country we live in. You say the Calumniators of California living at the Origon defeat their object in their own writings. Such may be the case among us who live here, but its far otherwise among the very millions who read these papers in Eng. & U.S. You know California and Californians as well as any other Person and can well describe both. I am bound to write to the Department of State quarterly. Last year I forwarded 15 to 20 letters. My opportunities of sending letters home are by every Vessel bound from this to Mazatlan. There my correspondent forwards to Vera Cruz and receive all my dispatches & private letters from V. C., paying the Post both ways. In this manner under cover to me the several supercargoes here receive these letters, there friends paying the U.S. postage and sending by U.S. mail their letters to N.Y. or N[ew]. O[rleans]. for the Vera Cruz packet. In this way you can order your letters.

I would advice you at your leasure hours to write a chapter or two, heading California, such a date, merely directing Sir, and signing any fictitious name you like. These send open to me as I should, if you please, like to read them. Per every opportunity I will send them to the U. S. to some Editor whose paper I take. I have just read several pages in the St. Louis paper, signed Pioneer (wrote I think by Mr Hastings), respecting this country, pretty well discribed. I now send to you some seven N. O. papers to April 26. I have no doubt but Texas now belongs

---

15 The subject was mentioned in Marsh's letter to Larkin dated Aug. 12, 1845, Pueblo of St. Joseph, and printed by Hammond, III, 308-310. Marsh did not respond to this second appeal from Larkin to write about California until Feb. 1, 1846, when he wrote his celebrated and widely printed letter to Senator Cass. This was not exactly "soon after receiving Larkin's request" (as Lyman claims, p. 270) even at the tempo of those leisurely days.

to the U. S. I do not believe that Commissioners are yet on their way to the Origon. By my last dates, Mr Packingham, English minister, was in Washington to settle the question. I think the officers of the America had quite a warm & keen feeling on the subject. When we find a Brother of Aberdeen & son of Peel in company we can not wonder at it. I consider that Peal and Aberdeen hold more power over the whole world than the united strenght of any three or four kings or Empires.

I am yours,
Thomas O. Larkin

III. Increased Consular Activity and Rumors of War

October 1845 - February 1846

BY THE autumn of 1845 rumors of war between the United States and Mexico and of a change in California's political status had become frequent, and Larkin's correspondence reported many of these rumors. His consular business became so complicated that he appointed William A. Leidesdorff to act as his vice-consul in Yerba Buena and gave him detailed instructions on how to conduct his office. At times Larkin becomes rather sententious, and some of his letters to Leidesdorff more than slightly resemble the advice of Polonius to Laertes. He told Leidesdorff not to worry about the failure of the British vice-consul, James Forbes, to recognize him. Forbes was already beginning to arouse Larkin's suspicions on account of his active support of the idea that Great Britain should take over California.

Larkin's letter to Dr. Elijah White displays his broadly humane outlook. Although Grove Cook was an American citizen, Larkin wished the Indian tribe Cook had wronged to have justice and due compensation, and he wanted Cook to stand trial for murder. Sutter's Fort was within Larkin's sphere of jurisdiction, and Sutter himself had not been willing or able to deal adequately with Cook or other unruly Americans who subscribed to the doctrines that the only good Indian was a dead one and that Europeans were not much good either.

Larkin continued to find time for his business affairs. He also consolidated his landholdings by getting Governor Pico to confirm the grant of a tract in the Sacramento Valley made by Governor Micheltorena to Larkin's children (who had been born in California and who therefore were "citizens" by Mexican law) and by purchasing other land outright, in his own name, from the Mexican grantees. Larkin's fortune was by this time considerable, and his financial prospects were

34

very bright indeed if only political stability would come to Alta California.

In the last letter of this section the name of Captain John Charles Frémont is mentioned. It is a name that will figure very prominently in the remainder of this correspondence. On February 8, 1846 (the date of the letter), Frémont, on his third Pacific Coast expedition, had recently visited Larkin at Monterey and was supposed to be on his way back to the United States via Fort Helvetia and the still disputed "Origon" country. The settlement of the Oregon question, reported to Leidesdorff on Stearns's authority in that same letter of February 8, had not, in fact, yet taken place.

[Larkin to Stearns, S. Coll.]

Monterey Oct 1, 1845

Mr Abel Stearns
Pueblo de Los Angeles
Sir

Mr Charles Kieger, a clerk of Mr Parrott, will visit your port in Captain Fisher's Vessel, bound to Mazatlan. He wishes to take with him as a present, a quantity of your grapes. Will you please have a Box or Basket put safe for him, for which he will pay you when he sees you.

You will also oblige me by Sending a Box or Basket of your best grapes (if two or three qualities send them) put up for me and mark them Mott Talbot & Co. with a letter to them in my name, and give them to Mr Kieger.

We are here waiting for the war news. "Under which Ring Besonio. Speak or die."[1] We hardly know what we are to be. I have no doubt but Texas is a part and parcel of the U.S. and the Origon is to be.

I at times send Mr Jones papers to read requesting him to forward to you or Mr Potter matters reaching Eng[land]. Aberdeen came out strong & had also Peele. I was lately in company with the Brother of the first and son of the second. They too were warm for origon. If M. & U.S. goes to war for any lenght of time, say a year, I suppose C. will be cut off from one Republic to be added to another on declaring peace and returning the Country to its legal & rightfull owners. The whole face of C. and its Inhabitants would be changed, making the redelivery

---

[1] An obvious misquotation from Shakespeare's *The Merchant of Venice*.

of no benefit to Mexico. If we must be taken let it be by a respectable force and kept so, not over run by we don't know who. After all at some 30 yrs hence [?] Columbia & California had better be a [word undecipherable] & free state within itself.

Two or three Companies of U.S. Dragoons have left Independence Miss. for the Origon. The French papers say the English were sending a squadron.

I am Respectifully
Thomas O. Larkin

Fama at S. Francisco uncertain
Tasso is at Santa Cruz bound up
California San Luis   "   "
D. Quixote San F. bound here 10 days
Sterling   "   "   "   "   5   "
Admittance "   "   "   "   5   "
Fisher's Brig "   "   "   "   10   "
U.S.S. Portsmouth 26 guns left yesterday for Mazatlan.
U.S.S. Levant from Oahu daily expected here
U.S.S. Savannah from Oahu to Callio expected this month.

We had but 3 Whalers, 1 English, 1 French, & 1 American.
Tallow is very abundant at the North. Wheat some.

An Accupulco Brig with Ponchos is here. Supercargo D. Domingo. Idart of A— says he did tell where he was going for fear of mighty troops. There was 4 Vessels & about 1000 soldiers in a ready. The Gen had not arrived tho' Idart had seen him somewhere [word undecipherable] provissions. Jose M. Castarneres passed on to Mexico. His wife was in a [three words obliterated] many Frenchmen. Mechanics I believe with the soldiers.

It is hard to say whether these Troops come or not.

[Larkin to White, LE 74]

Consulate of the United States of
America Port of San Francisco Novbr. 1, 1845

Sir

Having some Government Buisness to settle at this place, I came here in the United States ship Levant, Hugh N. Page Esqr Commander. During my being here, I find much anxiety to bring about a settlement for the Cattle left here by the Freinds of the Chief who was inhumanly shot by Grove Cook at the Establishment of Captain Sutter.

In the month of August last, I wrote an answer to yours pr Mr Climan,[2] and sent it to this place, to be forwarded to you by H. B. M. Ship America, bound as I supposed to the Columbia River. Capt Gordon objected to receiving it, saying it saying [sic] he was not bound there. It now remains at the English Vice Consuls who will send it with this my letter of to day to Capt Sutter and his answer, if he answers it. I much regret my first letter not going.

I must now request you to see the Father of the Person murdered, and the Chief of the tribe. Say to them that since the murder has become known throughout Calafornia, Grove Cook receives no favour, that all who are acquainted with the particulars regrets the circumstances, that the settlers on the Sacramento River when called on, will make good the number of Cattle or property lost, and that I have every reason to beleive now I have brought the affair to the notice of Governor Pico, that the murderer will be apprehended and be made to stand his trial. As we are three months some times hearing from the Government and your communication to Washington had to be translated, you will understand why I have no answer from him and also I am now several days from my consulate.

You will also offer my assistance to the party concerned. Give a passport to a sufficient number to come direct to Captain Sutter, or Monterey if neccessary, for their Cattle and property, and to make any legal demand through me or otherwise to this Government. You will endeavour to have only enough men come to Calafornia to protect themselves on the road and to drive the Cattle away. Do not have a number as to cause mistrust here that they had any other view, and give them my word they will be safe, well received and their claims satisfactory adjusted.

I am Sir with much
respect Your Obt
Thomas O. Larkin

Mr E. White
U. S. Sub Agent
for Indian affairs
    Origon.

---

[2] James Clyman, surveyor and fur trapper. Born in Virginia. First came to California in 1845. Lived in Napa till his death in 1881. See Bancroft, II, 762, and *James Clyman: American Frontiersman, 1792-1881*, ed. Charles L. Camp (San Francisco, 1928).

[Larkin to Yount, LE 74]

Yerba Buena Novbr 12th 1845.

Mr Yount[3]

Sir

Sr Guerero, the Sub Prefecto of this place, has promised me that in case any American Citizens will apply through William A. Leidesdorff Esqr (whom I have appointed U. S. Vice Consul for this place) that he will give them a passport to remain in this country untill they can receive passports from a higher authority. You will please make this known emidiately.

Your obt Servt
Thomas O. Larkin

[Larkin to Leidesdorff, LE 81]

Consulate of the United States
Monterey California Nov 22, 1845

Sir.

With this I send thirty passports, making altogether fifty that you will have received. I also send a copy of consular instructions for your information and government, and some large wafers with cut papers for your consular Seal.

I am waiting for your written acceptance of the appointment I have offered, and verbally accepted by you. Also send those certificates at Mr Forbes.

You will endorse on each passport and take a certificate of citizenship as pr copies I now forward. Have the certificates signed before you and be careful that no person but an American citizen obtains from you a passport, as there is a liability of one hundred dollars in the fact of giving a passport to a person known to be an alien, and deprivation of office.

You will observe in the consular instructions particular orders respecting our mode of conduct towards our countrymen and the authori-

---

3 George C. Yount, fur trapper. Native of North Carolina. Came to California with the Wolfskill party in 1831. He later worked for Vallejo at Sonoma. Obtained rancho in Napa Valley and prospered. Died in Napa in 1865. See Bancroft, V, 783, and Camp, "The Chronicles of George C. Yount, California Pioneer of 1826," *Calif. Hist. Soc. Quart.*, II (1923), 3-66, including a bibliography, p. 66.

ties of the country we live in, which must be of the most conciliatory character both for our official influence and to coincide with the policy of our government at home.

> I am with every respect
> Your most Obt
> Thomas O. Larkin

To
William A. Leidesdorff Esqr
U.S. Vice Consul.

[Larkin to Leidesdorff, LE 82]

Consulate of the United States of America
Monterey, California November 25 1845

Sir

Your communication by Mr Mellus was rec'd last night. You place to much importance respecting the non acknowledgement of your office by Mr Forbes. As to his saying he has not received any notice from the Supreme Goverment of Mexico, or from this Department of California, respecting your appointment, thats nothing. I do not expect he ever will. Excepting seeing my name in a Mexican paper naming my appointment, he has no other information of my commission. The same respecting his knowledge of the French Consulship of this country—I shall by no means give Mr Forbes official Notice of your appointment. By Section 7, page 22 & 23 in your Book of Instructions, you will see the power given U. S. Consuls to appoint Vice Consuls. That I am U. S. Consul of California, by authority of President Tyler, my commission will show, and the Mexican & California Government are well informed on the subject. It will be 10 or 12 months before I have answers to my letters to Washington relative to your appointment, and as the power of appointing you is invested in me, the appointment will in time be conformed by the State Department at Washington.

Again its a matter only of politeness and good feeling and Neighborliness between you two what Mr Forbes may say or think on the subject. The Authorities of your place know you as U. S. Vice Consul. All our Commanders of Ships of War or private ships will acknowledge you as such, and you must wait a 8 or 10 months for full acknowledgment. Whatever your Neighbor may tell you about his correspondence with the Departments in London, you may believe his correspondence goes only to Mr Barron, who may send extracts to England if he considers the matter of sufficient importance.

In all letters or verbal correspondence with the English Vice Consul of your port be very gaurded. In fact I know of little business officially you need have with him. Respecting the seaman, I know of no right he had in the case with the Captain. Any Seaman under our Flag enjoys its protection. On the other hand, if he has signed the articles, no power can take him out against the consent of the Consul or Captain. Should he not have signed the Articles, the A^m Consul, not any other, must take him out, if the man actually asks his assistance. As I have before told you, time only will teach you the duties of your office. You will however freely write to me and often respecting any case or in want of any information.

> I am Yours
> respectifully
> Thomas O. Larkin

William A. Leidesdorff Esq
U. S. Vice Consul
San Francisco

[Larkin to Leidesdorff, LE 85]

> Consulate of the United States
> Monterey. December 6, 1845

Sir.

Yours pr Srs Aguirre & Pedrorena I have received. I am sorry to hear that you have so much vexsation on taking office. Respecting what Mr Forbes may say, you think to much on. By my letter per Mr Belden you will find that Mr F has not been officially informed of my appointment, only seing it in a Newspaper. Nor will he be. He has, I am told, the year back disputed my appointment only as a Vice for this port only—this made no difference to me. As to the non acknowledgement of the Authorities of the place you live in of your office, you must get on as you can. The Prefect will, on his arrival here, write to the sub prefect. I have wrote to the Governor, who will give the Alcade of 1845 the proper information. Respecting your Alcade of 1845, if you can do no business with him, leave it undone. In time the acknowledgements from every quarter from Yerba Buena to Washington will come to us.

Mr Forbes's appointment coming from Mr E. Barron, who took time to receive the acknowledgement from Mexico, before he sent it, gave time for the information to be general before the Vice Consul began to act. Mr Barron and myself hold the same rank of office, originating from his King and our President, both having power to appoint Vice Consuls. Mr Forbes holds from the Consulate of San Blas, you from the Consulate of Monterey. My jurisdiction extends to half way to any other U.S. Consul in the Republic of Mexico. My right over your appointment or any other Vice Consulate in California you will find in your Consular Instructions, page 22, Section 7, Article 40 & 41.

Respecting the right or power of Captain Hinckley to imprison and fine Men, or ship them, I should say that if he chooses to imprison and fine a seaman for Deserting, I would allow him to do so, if his laws allows him to do it, as it may prevent Desertions here after in your port. But he must not put American Seamen at public works in the streets, nor ill treat, or badly feed them. You as Consul, can not allow any Am Seaman to be forced on board any ship to go to Sea against his will, either to pay a fine or any other purpose, more particular a Foreign Ship.

Should any seaman allow your Captain of the Port to ship him, he can do so. So can your Cook, if the Am Seamen is willing, and unless *you* sign the articles, this same Seaman can at the next port leave the Ship, and before any U. S. Consul claim the highest wages of that Port for the 90 days previous. No shipment or discharge of a man from any Am Vessel while in your port is legal or valid unless done before you. The same here, yet I never care if an Am Captain ships a man without my knowledge. Thats his look out and risk, not mine. This man can go to you for a clearance, should he arrive at your port and wish to leave. The same here, should any man claim my assistance to take him out of a Vessel from Capt H. shipping him. Therefore, let them do so. Time will remedy these affairs, and each one will learn his relative duties. Yet you will continue writing on these and other subjects, and should any Am Captain wish you to ship or discharge one man or many, you will charge him 50 cts for each discharge, & 1$ for each man shipt, with two dollars for the Certificate whether you mention one man's name or twenty. To Captains of Foreign Vessels who choose to give you business, you will charge Mexican fees, if you can find out what they are. You will find your Consular agency go on well in time. I myself give a poor man his fee if he asks it, but not a Captain of a Vessel, yet I allow him to do his business without my knowledge should he wish to do so in order to gain or save the value of the fee. I hold my office for security of property, and because its an honourable one, not for the sake of fees, yet will charge them when due, but do not care how few papers are brought to me, only the Register. And that may prehaps be left any time (say for the voyage) if the Captain dont like to pay 4$ too often. I hope you may gain honour, name, respectibility, and increase of business by the appointment, but not have a single dispute about a fee, or with any one of our countrymen. I saw on board the Hibernia, Captain Smith, two sawyers, who Mr Green sent up to the woods this side of the Pueblo with two saws, axes, tools, pots &c, and advance wages, 50 or 60$. All this they stole or sold, and ran to Y. B., yet I let them remain on board and said nothing, rather than weaken the Hibernian crew, or have a dispute with the Captain. Had I been a private man, I would had them out.

Did you settle with Capt. Barnum. I have paid off his two men their extra wages. Did you notice 3$4 againt him for postage.

Yours respectifully
Thomas O. Larkin

Send me those 10 Certificats of Mr Forbes.

[Larkin to Leidesdorff, LE 87]

Monterey December 12 1845

Sir—

I have now officially informed the Governor, Don Pedro Narvaez,[4] and the Administrador of your appointment. They will in a short time inform the Authorities of Yerba Buena. Pr first opportunity I shall notify the Department of State and our Minister in Mexico.

As John Smith agreed to work for you to pay me 103$ in hides, and you promised to secure the amt. providing he gained that much, I shall not take other measures to obtain the payment. Should he fail to come to you in Jan. or you have debts against him (and I understood you, there was none to be in my way), I wish you to make it your business to have some one on the River collect it by force, as he is aiming for the Columbia. It being in your hands, I hope by work or otherwise you will collect the debt.

I want you by first Boat [to] send up to Captain Sutter's Rancho, prehaps his upper Rancho is best, two fanagas of good Beans and Four

---

4 Pedro Narvaez, Mexican naval lieutenant; military commandant at Monterey in 1845. Bancroft, IV, 752.

Bags of best Potatoes for planting. Have them in strong Bags, well sewed up, marked and directed, one half to Henry Buker [?], the other half to James Meadows. Write to the two men that you send them, enclosing the letters in one to Capt. Sutter, requesting him to notify the owners. Send me a Bill of the above.

The Governor has shipt D. Jose A. Carrillo[5] and one or two others on board the Clara for Mexico for being in engaged in a rise. The people in the Pueblo are in favor of Pico. Those in San B. have voted in favor of Castro. So they may go. Thats not our business, tho' I wish they would all rise together to help the Country in its troubles.

I am &c
Thomas O. Larkin

[Parrott to Leidesdorff, LE 88]

Mazatlan Decr 15th 1845

My Dear Leidesdorff

Your letter pr the Levant has been received. I cannot have made here the Seals you require for you[r] Consulate. The Engraver is not now here, but will endeavor to do so by the next opportunity.

Since my return I have bought the Brig Hannah, which vessel I send to Monterey on business, and in the mean time, I have instructed the Super Cargo, Mr Ajuria to pick up a full cargo of tallow for her, provided he can get it for Bills. I send no money not being certain so late in the Season of getting a cargo. However, should the Brig go to your Port and there be tallow, Mr. Ajuria will make you acquainted with the terms. He will pay 11 Rs in Bills on M, Tepic, Guadalajara, Mexico or Lima but only in the Case of a Security of getting a full cargo or nearly so will he take any. The Hannah, I think, will carry as much as the Matador. She is 152 tons, a Beautiful Craft.

I am happy to state that there will not be any War between this and the United States. The expedition for California is at Acapulco. I mean the Chartered ships. This Government will never be able to send it off. It has no means and less energy. All the vessels are gaining high freights, and the Crews of many are down with the fever.

There is an expectation of a change of Govt. and a revolution every moment in Mexico.

---

5 José Antonio Ezequiel Carrillo. Bancroft, II, 745-746.

I know of nothing that would interest you further. To Larkin I send lots of news papers from the U. S. I presume he will send some to his agent at San Franco.

Wishing you health and prosperity I remain your friend,

Sincerely
John Parrott

P. S. If you should see Mrs Stephens give her my respects, not before her husband, however.

[Larkin to Stearns, S. Coll.]

Monterey December 30 1845

Mr Abel Stearns
Sir—

Your letter informing me of the passing of the Land tittles of four Ranchos I have received and thank you for your kind attentions. The passing of these land papers will cause a favourable opinion on the part of the new Owners and many others, towards Governor Pico. Mr McKinley had lead me to believe that not a Foreigner who had rec'd Ranchos from Gen. M. Micheltorena would receive an approval from the Legislature in the Pueblo. My believe from this was so small, that I left out the names of two or three Persons who had rights to offer. The same favour for them I must ask in this letter.

Viz.   Francisco Job Dye, Josefa Sota (Wife of James Stokes), E. Grimes.

On the 15 of December 1844 [General Micheltorena] gave a Rancho of five leagues on the River Sacramento, above Captain Sutter, runing back two leagues to my children Francisco, Carolina Ana, and Sofia Adelaida,[6] which will be found in Book of "Despacho en el Lebro respectivo a jojas 8."

I know not the right to naturalize children to young and give them land. Yet both was done as the General powers were all powerfull. I suppose it will be considered right. Again in California the tenor of the laws often give ways to conveyance or the State of affairs among us. In asking for the approval of these Farms, this one may pass, like the

---

[6] Larkin's famous Mexican "Children's Ranch" grant was finally recognized as valid by the U.S. courts after much anxious delay.

others. Should it not, you will please use your influence to effect its passage. In fact, I do not suppose the case will be noticed among others. Here I never know it to be.

You will please give to Mr Howard's particular charge the titles of all these Farms, after you have obtained the approval of these four. Mr Hartnell also has one, and would be obliged to you to have it brot forward tho' he had not told me to say so. I wish you would drawn on me for 4 or 5$ each for the Fees or expences of these writings, and ask Mr Howard to cash the draft. The value of the Alcahol I suppose he paid you.

Your attention to this business will obliged.

Yours Respt
Thomas O. Larkin

I heard Mrs Cooper say yesterday in talking of oranges, "Well Don Abel has never as yet sent me an orange. Its now time to ask him."

[On back of letter: Should you have any arrival from San Blas, or Mazatlan, please take chge of all papers for me, and send them to me by safe Persons.]

[Larkin to Stearns, S. Coll.]

Monterey December 30 1845

Mr Abel Stearns
Sir—

I hardly know what to think of the news mentioned in your letter by Don Valle,[7] that you had from the Frenchman saying the war between Mexico & U. S. was published in Mazatlan September 2d. If so why have we not news in some certain way. The Mexican Ports may be so blockaded by the Savannah, Warren, Portsmouth and Levant, all whom was I think at Mazatlan between Sept. & Decr that no vessel could have been sent here by Mexico. Yet I should suppose that Com. Sloat would had to have informed me if there was war between our country and any other Nation. There are others ways also of our hearing of such important news during three months. Mexico was compromised

---

7 Ignacio del Valle, son of Antonio del Valle. Came to California from Jalisco in 1825. Held various military and government offices under the California provincial government and was appointed treasurer of the civil government by Governor Pico. Also held office after the American conquest. Died in 1880. Bancroft, V, 755-756.

by her oft pledged word, and by National Honour, to declare word [war?] on Texas becoming one of the U.S. That such had happened we can not doubt, yet those who hold the honour of Mexico in their hands may have personal interest in to high a degree to think of their countrys weal or Welfare. They as well as ourselfs, must be aware that in a War with the U.S. they must lose other Departments in place of gaining the one they aim for. What is the private or public opinion your way of the Foreign Emigration at the Sacrimento. In October 50 Waggons with 4 to 500 Durham Cows and 300 Men, Women & Children arrived at or near Capt. Sutter. There are many Germans among these Imigrants, more than any one would believe. If this Government do not settle some of these new comers, the other side of the San Joaquin, this country will soon be ruined. The killing of the whites this way is near one a month. A Mexican and an Englishman have been killed near M. within 3 months. I'm not a grumbler, yet do not like the state of the country. Its more as they had it in 35, a Gov. and a Gen. being in all cases one to many. Two heads can not rule neither a man, Animal or country. The affairs must be conducted by one. Add to this, the country is about to be distracted in the question of the Capital. Now the Comissaria, by & by the Aduana. Both your Town and Monterey will with the big ones, keep up this affair to the distruction of many better interest. Of course I want things as they were. You of course want a removal of Government and gov't patronage to the Pueblo. I can only say in favour of M. this was the Capital, and the country must be distracted in the removal. If it had always been in some other place, I would say the same of its removal. You may tell me you care not where it is. Family—Pride —interest, love of the place you live in, forbids one to believe the assertion if made. Prehaps should the time ever come when there is no Aduana, there will be no Revolution—and each one will get his own living. Your Gov. had made himself strong by the shipment of his two Neigbors. More than 200 Soldiers would make him. As you have the Gov, the Tribunal, 6/7 of the Deputies and all there Seconds, you ought to make some head way in geting 9/10 of the loaves and fishes. The good of the Country is not so pressing. In fact, what is the good of the country but the good of its people, and what is the latter's good but let them get all they can. You Southerners are now the People. Ergo, you ought to have the Aduana. Those of the North have had it long enough—prehaps. For my part, I have become so accostomed to being a Government Contracter, I suppose I must follow the Government. Ergo, I'll have a House in the Pueblo as well as in M. Therefore shall always be in the Capital, and can then very quietly sit down and see the said Loaves & fishes fall or swim whenever the like, or the People likes to have them, knowing whenever it rains I always get as wet as I choose to.

I was not aware that Sr Abrego had tendered his resignation untill Sr Valle arrived here. Why he done so, dont know, but it appeard the resigning of the sineus of war, and the pleasures of peace to a man from below could not for a minute be thought of. He must therefore return to those who sent him. Had his mission not been to carry away all, even the Com^t General two thirds to your part of the world, prehaps it might pass, but all was to much. In fact they found it would be all, in every sense of the word.

Can there no way be found that the civil and military can fail [to] obtain their proper & respective share, and then take care of the Country. I am sorry Gov Pico did not commission me to receive his one third and send it to him. Don Pablo told me he had in August concluded to do so, but on second thought concluded the 5 pr cent too much, so lost the whole. I could I think with all ease sent him at one time 8000$ of the Matador's cargo that D. Jose Abrego retain a long time for him, the Super cargoes refusing to take it, tho' want of forms, receipts, cerrimony, or something or other, and could tomorrow ship him more. Its possible that it may be supposed that my interest would not allow me to attend to the Governor's, altho' on entering the Cargo of the Matador, I knew I was to take in public & private debts 8000$ of the goods. I rose the prices 25 to 50 pr ct, losing myself 2000$ by the operation, for one quarter the amt. my com^s, yet I did so because its my policy to serve those who employ me, it in the long run, much produce me more business—20 times 5 pr ct. brings me the whole Capital. I would not sell goods for others for 20 pr ct. could I make this arangement. I believe it would prove satisfactory to his Ex^c and I think tho' my way of doing business, my influence, and the willingness of those here, that when there was an entry, the Gov. would receive his part in Cash, hides or goods as the case may be. On entering the Brig now here duties 19,500$, two Merchants were called in, and put a fair price on the goods. Since then Don Pablo has allowed a rise of 20 to 30 pr cent, making a difference to me of 500 or 800$, if I take what is offered me. This Brig, Danish, Supercargo a Brother of Don Cesario, on arriving here, handed in her papers to Mr Hartnell, Don Pablo being on his third trip to your place. It was accertain that her duties amounted to 20,000, having only six articles White 40 yds ps. Manta, Creas, Muslin, Callico, Broadcloth, & Cassimere. 2500$ was offered in Cash. Each one I suppose will be allowed by & by to offer what they choose. On Don P.

being sent for, two merchants were chosen to price the goods. As I had much interest in the result, viz, taking goods for pay, and not wanting any one to obtain such prices as I obtained for Mr Parrott, I refused. The cloth was put at 8$. Cassimere at 2$4. Callico at 12 to 14—on these terms the Vessel *would* enter. She did enter, by paying 2000$ Cash here, 2000$ to Sʳ Alvarado in Mazatlan and the remainded in goods— I now find Callico has been raisd to 15$, Cassimere 3$5, cloth 10$4, 2ᵈ quality 8$4. Why I know not. Some says because Sʳ A. is to have 1500$ more than was agreed on in Cash. Don Pablo informs that the rise was made because he charged more duties than Mr H. did, yet the duties is 19500$, or more duties than Don C. & Brother expected to pay. Why I much be charged on 2000 or 3000$ 20 or 25 for 4 more, that Mr A. may have more money, or to please Don C., the Deponent said not.

I suppose Mr Mellish will bring up an order for 10 or 12000$ from the Governor, payable out of the Barnsable. Whether it will pass, time will say. If the Government owes you, and you can do no better, send to me the Governor's order for it, and direction what I kind of pay to take, and if you do not ask for too much cash, I think I can Collect it for you, which shall be done without expence. For all I may be able to do for you I rarely ask for money. This year have not I believe rec'd a dollar from Government in Cash.

Don Juan B. Alvarado intends to proceed to Mexico by the first opportunity after Jan or Feb. I may consider it of more importance than you do, that he should go. I think you will believe me in my saying I have wrote to you quite enough this time. Have you seen my two sons this month in the Pueblo. We have light rains for the last 8 or 10 days, sufficient for ploughing. There is more flour in M. than any year sinc 40, and all fine. Don Pedro's Mill in the Pueblo turns out four a[rrobas] fine flour to the fan. of Wheat—its worth here 12 to 14 Rials cash. Beans 5$, trade Corn 4$ do, Barley 2$4 & 3$ do.—Corn is scarce. Beans plenty for the price—Did Mr Jones send you Newspaper 3 or 4 times.

I am yrs with respect—
Thomas O. Larkin

[Larkin to Leidesdorff, LE 101b]

Monterey 8 of Feb 1846

Captain W. A. Leidesdorff
Sir.

Captain Philps[8] has arrived at San Pedro 136 days from Boston, dispatched by the owners of the Sterling. We look for him every day.* Scott Wilson's vessel is to arrive here this week to take the flag, then sails for Mazatlan with the cargo of the Danish Brig "Maria."

The Brig Hanna, or Hannah, has arrived at San Diego from Mr Parrott. She comes for Tallow. The Origon question, Mr Stearns informs me, is settled in favor of the U. S.—also the Texas question, both without war. We have a Special Minister in Mexico to arrainge affairs. The U. S. have five ships of war in Mazatlan & three times that number in Vera Cruz. By the conveyance of this letter, I send one to Mr Weber for Capt. Fremont.[9] We have some rain every 48 hours.

I am Yours Respectibely
Thomas O. Larkin

*Bark Moscow

---

8 William D. Phelps. Native of Massachusetts. Came to California in 1840. Master of the *Alert*, 1840-42. Master of the *Moscow*, 1846. Wrote *Fore and Aft* (Boston, 1871), an account of his life at sea and in California. Living in Lexington, Mass., in 1872. Bancroft, IV, 775-776.

9 Frémont had returned to New Helvetia about January 15 and had visited Monterey on January 27. He was to raise the American flag on Gavilán Peak on March 5 or 6.

IV. Stormy Petrels:
Hastings, Frémont, and Gillespie

March-June 1846

"THE thundering wheels of time" were now rolling in California, given an assisting shoulder by Lansford Warren Hastings as well as by Thomas Jefferson Farnham. Frémont had flown the Stars and Stripes over a fortified position on Gavilán Peak early in March 1846, but after this foolhardy gesture of defiance toward General Castro's Mexicans, Frémont had retreated northward—in Larkin's words "queiteley presing his way to the Oregon." But within a month another exciting visitor arrived in Monterey, Lieutenant Archibald H. Gillespie of the United States Marine Corps, with a secret dispatch for Larkin from the Secretary of State. This famous document, drawn up on October 17, 1845, took six months to reach Larkin, and he had already "anticipated" some of its instructions before he read it. The series of letters he sent to his friends and confidants among the Americans in California (two of them are printed here; others are to be found in *The Larkin Papers*) indicates clearly how he meant to carry out his plans for a peaceful acquisition of California by the United States. This was to be achieved with the full knowledge and approval of its leading Mexican inhabitants, after a declaration of independence. The fear that Britain instead of the United States would be first on the scene still troubled Larkin unduly, as his "anticolonialism" letter of May 1, 1846, clearly shows. He also reacted suspiciously toward the arrival of the "Rev Mr Macnamara" at Monterey early in June with plans to settle "ten thousand Irish in C." on behalf of the London Emigration Society.

The cloak-and-dagger nature of Gillespie's mission is indicated by mysterious references to "Mr. A. H. G." and "Mr. G." in Larkin's letters to Leidesdorff at this time. Gillespie was now on his way north

50

on his forced march to overtake Frémont and to deliver to him messages from Senator Thomas Hart Benton, Frémont's father-in-law. Captain Montgomery with the U.S.S. *Portsmouth* was standing by in San Francisco Bay. Larkin was anxious to collect every scrap of news from the Sacramento Valley, where the "emigrates from the U.S." were pouring in and the Mexicans were said to be challenging the right of foreigners to hold land. "The pear" was certainly "near ripe for falling."

Meanwhile the junta, or Committee of Safety, summoned by Governor Pico to meet at Santa Barbara on June 15, was confidently expected to declare Alta California independent. Larkin made preparations to be in Santa Barbara at the time but decided not to arrive in a United States naval vessel for fear of alarming the Californians. The previous junta had met in April at his own house in Monterey, and he was on good terms with nearly all the delegates chosen to go to Santa Barbara.

[Hastings to Marsh, Ma. Coll. CSL]

New Helvetia, March 26th, 1846[1]

Dear Sir,

Although an entire stranger to you personally, yet I have had the honor of knowing you by reputation during the last several years, which fact I hope, Sir, you will have the goodness to receive as a sufficient apology for my thus addressing you without the ordinary preliminary of a formal introduction. Nothing, I assure you, Sir, could afford me greater pleasure than to see you personally and to have the honor of making your valuable acquaintance; but existing circumstances appear to deny me that honor.

As you may perhaps have learned, I arrived in this country in December last, with a view of visiting Oregon by the earliest opportunity, but as no opportunity has thus far presented, I have now changed my purpose and determined to go as far back as Green river or Bridger's Fort, with the view of conducting the emigrants to this country by a better and more direct route than that usually traveled. The change of purpose above alluded to will prevent my visiting any portion of the lower country until my return, which will be some time in the month of August or September next, when, Sir, you can rely upon an acces-

---

[1] Compare the letter that Hastings wrote to Larkin on March 3, 1846, in Hammond, IV, 220-221.

sion of six or seven thousand human souls, to our foreign population in California. This is the very least estimate that can be made; for, judging from the universal excitement which pervades almost every portion of the Union, the emigration will be much more likely to amount to fifteen or twenty thousand. And the emigration of this year is only a prelude to what is to follow in succeeding years, for California is now looked upon among a large majority of our people as the *garden of the earth*. No one will doubt but that this is perfectly right; for our people have undoubtedly the same right that other foreigners or even the Californians themselves have, to locate in and enjoy this delightful country, conforming always to the established and existing laws.

I brought a letter, which I discover among others, for you from your old friend T. J. Farnham Esq., but as I have had no opportunity of forwarding it directly to you, I have thought proper to defer sending it until now, as the presumption is that it contains facts and statements which are not designed for the public eye, and which should not be placed into the hands or under the control of strangers or enemies to the cause of *freedom*. Friend Farnham is doing every thing in his power to increase the emigration to this far-famed region, and he is of the opinion that he will be able to bring at least three or four thousand from the State of New York alone. But there are many other states which will do much more than the state of N. York. Ohio, my native state, will send her thousands annually, and Kentucky, Indiana, Illinois, Michigan, Missouri, Tennessee, and Arkansas will not be far in the rear. As to the natural, the inevitable result of this unprecedented emigration to the western World, I need not trouble you with my own speculations, for the result must have been long since anticipated by your self.

I hope, Sir, the false impression that our people design to wrest this country forcible from the Californians will not be promulgated, and if promulgated, I sincerely hope that it will not be credited by either the Californians or others, for it is not true. But on the contrary, they design to emigrate to this country, with a settled purpose to comply with all just laws and reasonable governmental requirements, and above all things, as far as I am able to learn, they come with a settled purpose also, to cooperate with the Californians in their opposition to any foreign encroachment upon their rights, whether that encroachment be by Mexico or any other power. In return for this cooperative aid they expect protection of both person and property, and they also expect equal rights, privileges and immunities. *But they can not be expelled from the country, nor must their expulsion be attempted!* What consummate folly it is for the natives of the Californias to attempt to check the emigration to this country. They might just as well attempt to arrest the thundering wheels of time, to restrain the mighty water's flow, or to extinguish the blazing light of civil and religious liberty!

In much haste, allow me to conclude by subscribing myself,

Your most obt. and humble Servt.
L. W. Hastings

To Dr. John Marsh

[Larkin to Stearns, S. Coll.]

Monterey March 26th 1846

Able Stearns Esqr
Dear Sir

By Captain Phelps[2] the Alcalde I sent you a translation of Captan J C Fremonts letter to me which was not correct.[3] A few days afterwards I forwarded you a correct one which you will please not use nor give any copy of unless the bad Translation has been received first, in which case it will be nessesary to correct it. Capt Phelps, when he left this place, said he was bound for San Pedro direct, but a few days since I have learned he was in the bay of San Francisco. The Don Quixote entred a small cargo last week. The Vandalia sails to morrow for San Francisco & the Hamburg Bark Alferd for San Pedro. The Barnstable has not arrived yet. Mr. Mellus is here waiting. All Troubles have passed over. Capt Fremont is queiteley presing his way to the Oregon or elsewhere according to his instructions from home.

I am yrs & c
Thomas O. Larkin

---

[2] William D. Phelps.

[3] Also referred to in Hammond, IV, 260 (Larkin to Stearns, March 19, 1846), where the nature of the bad translation is explained.

[Larkin to Leidesdorff, LE 123]

Monterey April 19th 1846[4]

Sir.

Allow me the pleasure of introducing to your acquantance Mr Archibald H. Gillispie, a Gentleman well worthy of Attention. If you can do anything for his accommodation, you will confer a personal obligation on

Your Most Obt Sevt
Thomas O. Larkin

To William A. Leidsdorff Esqr
U. S. Vice Consul
San Francisco

[Howard to Stearns, S. Coll.]

Yerba Buena April 21, 1846

Abel Stearns Esq.
My Dear Sir

Rainy & cold as the old nick. The country however about here wants a little more rain and we shall have a most excellent year. I hope you are as well off at the leeward. We have news here of the Barnstable arrival at the leeward. Mellus is waiting at Monterey for her. Paty has arrived and gone to Acapulco chartered by Castro. He paid Larkin 6000$ and Larkin paid Paty $ 3000 down. Larkin has got his out of Davis, who has arrived with the Brig Euphemia with a fine assortment of goods. The Brig belongs to himself & E & H. Grimes.

A few days ago a "Coreo" left the Pueblo for Los Angl. with a representation to his Excellency the Gov. complaining of the Monterey Big Bugs—that they spend all the duties in "Bailes y Meriendas." Those Coveys have few friends up this way. I am afraid we shall see a great deal of trouble in California this year. There are 7 or 8000 emigrates from the U.S. expected and this Hastings who has written a book about California is determined, I think, to kick up a row. God forbid we should have any trouble this year. Larkin talks some of going home

---

4 Not in Hammond, but compare longer letter of same date addressed to Leidesdorff printed in Hammond, IV, 302.

with me in Jany accrost land. You had better make up your mind and go with us.

I intend to leave this for the leward in about a fortnight. Shall be in San Pedro about the last of May.

Please give my best respects to yr. family and beleive me

Yr^s very truly
W. D. M. Howard

[Larkin to Leidesdorff, LE 125]

Monterey April 23 1846.[5]

Captain W A Leidesdorff

Sir.

The Portsmouth, John B. Montgomery Esq., arrived here yesterday 21 days from Mazatlan. She should have waited another week for the Mexican mail, but was hurried away by my account of Capt. Fremont wrote previous to the letters that Captain Philps[6] deluded me out of and carried N in place of South. Our Minister has been refused in Mexico. By the Message of President Polk that I forwarded to you by W. H. Davis you find his reccommendation to do nothing with M. until the reception of our Mexican Minister was known. That is *now* known. And in all likelihood the States have declared War against M. to bring her to peace in proper time, in which case the com. may be weekly expected here. When Capt. M. left Mazatlan it was found that the Gov't there had very late news as the C.H. officers and other officers with all the archives had gone to Rosario and said that the A^m would soon declare the port in a state of Blockade which shows they were aware of some important news. As the sailing for C. of the Portsmouth was not known in Maz^t she only brought a few letters to me from Mr Parrott, and my home letters. I am sending a letter to Mr Archabald H. Gillespie with a few papers of N.Y. Feb. Should they not reach him at the Pueblo, I have ordered them to be sent to you and you will forward them to Capt Sutter for Mr Gillespie. Should opportunity not offer in

---

5 This letter differs in certain important particulars from that sent by Larkin to Gillespie on the same date and printed in Hammond, IV, 340-341, although the news that it conveys is similar. The very significant final paragraph of this letter finds no parallel in that to Gillespie. Leidesdorff acknowledged the receipt of this letter on April 25, as did Gillespie that of his on the same date (Hammond, IV, 346-348).

6 William D. Phelps.

4 days you will send them at my expense as cheap as possible. Read the papers and without having them go out of yr hands, carefully enclose them again. As I have no time to write this letter over or any other you will shew it to Mr Howard and Capt. Vincent.

There is every appearance of war with Mexico, none with Eng. Her Gov't is confused by the passing of the Corn laws. Peale was out 10 days, had to be recalled. Mr Packingham has 2 or 3 times offered Mr Buchanan to settle the Origon question (which our President refuses) by arbitration. The opening for grain is to be of much importance to the States who now ought to modify our Tariff for the benefit of Eng. If you are selling any Real Estate, hold on a time, and see if it may not bring more in /47.

By John H. Everett' letters of Decr 12[7] it appears at over 1000 Mormons are coming. I have no letters for or about Mr Howard's business of a new ship.

I am inclined to think some of the great ones here are preparing for the coming change. If so I hope the[y] will not allow their followers to be entirely in the dark. And after all, these reports may prove but squalls. Yet the pear is near ripe for falling.

Yrs. in haste—
Thomas O. Larkin

Send me yr a/c
Dr & Cr.

[Larkin to Leidesdorff, LE 127]

Monterey Apr 27, 1846[8]

William A. Leidesdorff Esqr.

Yours of the 25, I rec'd this afternoon. Say to Mr Howard I wrote a part of that letter to him and wished him to read the whole. As we daily

---

7 Printed in Hammond, IV, 118-121. In this long and very entertaining letter Everett writes: "Settle all your affairs promptly next spring. you will have all the Mormonry among you, who will act towards you as the Israelites did to the nations among whom they came, kill you all off & take possession of your worldly gear." Later he wrote, "One of todays papers says that are about 10,000 Mormons ready to start for California. . . ." Larkin reduced this estimate to "over 1000."

8 Except for the whole of the first paragraph and the whole of the P.S., this letter was previously printed in Catherine C. Phillips, *Portsmouth Plaza: The Cradle of San Francisco* (San Francisco, 1932), pp. 46-47. Here it is given in its entirety.

look for him, I do not now write to him. The Taylor says he has no
cloth of yours nor order to obtain any. I did not before understand the
business. I have now requested him to call on Capt. Paty's Nephew
this day and in my name obtain sufficient for a suit. Your private or
any a/c to first of this month you will send to me soon as opportunity offers. Respecting Mr G. by & by will answer. Should any person present himself to you this summer requesting means to find his
way to this office, and you should have reason to suppose the importance will warrent the expense, you will within the hour furnish him
with what he may need to arrive at my house.

I have wrote to Hon James Buchanan respecting yr appointment.
Shall have an answer in prehaps October. Of the result I have no doubt.
My several communications of 1845 have beene rec'd by our Govern-
ment in a remarkable flattering manner.

There is a prospect of a highly exciting times this or next year. The
want of War will retard but not prevent the forcoming events, events
sure to take place as day follows Night, and with the same beneficial
affect as the former brings after the latter. It will require bold heads
and steady minds and connected with every caution, care & produce
[prudence] to launch into the vortex. Follow the stream and profit by the
result. You must use every care as an officer to gaurd your words and
passion. Make it your business for the name and honor of the country
in whose employ you are not to enlist yourself in any [of] the petty
affairs of the town you reside in, but do you[r] utmost to pacify and
keep in good faith and humor the Natives around you. Keep on the best
possible terms with those of the country in office. Let not past or present
offences prevent it. Keep letters of this class to yourself. By all means
prevent our countrymen from trying to injure or browbeat the people
of the country. Be a pacifier between both, and in the end you will meet
your reward in seeing affairs brought to a happy conclusion and California flourishing as so fine a country must flourish.

I will from time to time keep you informed of any certain news I
may have. The Congress should be here in a few days to remain a week
and then proceed to Mazatlan, if there is no war. The Savannah leaves
Mazatlan for home in 15 or 20 days, curcumstances not preventing it.
The Portsmouth will visit your port. She remains on the coast some
months. You will do well to have some potatoes, cabbages &c that you
can supply her. If you can purchase a Bbl of *good Sperm* oil or two, do
so, for the ship. I presume you could dispose of some Salmon to the
office[r]s. Mr Gillespie was well please with your attention to him and
I have no doubt but the officers of all our ships who visit your place

will have reason to thank you for your fine house and its table & wine. All this I am aware will cost you a round sum, yet you are establishing yourself and in gaining a name will also gain a fortune. With care & produce you must go ahead, and the country is now opening wider than ever for men of action. Do not detail to strangers your petty quarrels with those around you. They of course will agree to much you tell them, yet care nothing about it. Nor tell them the prices of the wine and fruit they eat at your table. They care not they about that. I would not continue on bad terms with the English V. Consul, whenever you know he is willing to be on better. Should he, as I hear, do little or mean things to you do not retaliate. You soon will be far beyond his Ways or Malice and care nothing about him. I understand Mr Spence may be appointed British Consul. I hope it may prove so. In Aug or Sept. we expect the Columbus, 90 gun ship from Canton.

I am yours &c
Thomas O. Larkin

Give my respects to Mr Mactavish. You will oblige me by obtain a large spencimen of the ore of quick silver and sulpher from Sonoma.

[Larkin to Stearns, S. Coll.]

Monterey April 27th 1846

Mr Abel Stearns

With this conveyance you have the President's Message of Decr 2d 1845.[9] From this document you will perceive that Mr Polk has taken a high stand respecting the Oregon from which he will not decend. Mr Tyler had before said the Oregon is ours, and we shall people it. This operation is now in the full course of experiment. Mr Polk in Decr 1846 [1845] objected to do anything with Mexico relative to our many demands against that Nation untill one more Minister should have been sent to Mexico. Mr Slidel of La has now been there, and from my Mexican papers to March 12th or 14th and New York papers to February 25th, I find that Mr Slidel' Ministry has been refused. General Parades

---

9 Stearns's reply to this letter, dated May 14, 1846, acknowledging receipt of the President's message and the constitution of the state of Texas, has been printed by Hammond, IV, 374-375. The frequency with which Larkin wrote to Stearns during these days is remarkable. In addition to those letters printed here, others are in Hammond: May 21, IV, 385-386; May 23, IV, 389-390; May 24, IV, 391-393; and May 26, IV, 396.

has put out Herrera. The people are now puting him out. The Northern Departments of Mexico wish to seperate and become two Nations. The Portsmouth was on the 1st waiting for the last Mexican mail. The Commandante General of Mazatlan had a very late one (an express), when Commodore Sloat heard of Captain Fremonts situation and at once dispatched her for this Consulate jurisdiction. When the Portsmouth sailed, the Commandante General of Mazatlan had published a Bando, informing the Inhabitants that the Commodore would on the morrow declare the port in a state of Blocade (thereby giving the Americans reason to suppose that there was War, and the Commodore had the News), which he had not, but was expecting it. The Government Officers had left Mazatlan for Rosaria, taking the archives Etc., and all the National vessels left Mazatlan. The United States in January or February were determined to declare War against Mexico, unless, she herself declared the War, or came to terms. No two adjacent Nations can continue long as Mexico and the United States have been of late. War or better terms is the only alternative. Should the former now be the case, I beleive that the stars would shine over California before the 4th of July, blessing those who see it, and their posperity after them. Should peace continue (and it cannot as it is) it *must* be peace and Friendship, then the fate of this Country may be defered. It must, in my opinion, change by some means. Should my ideas be right, I hope the Natives of California will improve the opportunity. Rancheros may be bettered by the change, perhaps not the Merchants. I myself as a trader prefer everything as it is. The times and the country are well enough for me. I am partial to the people, and flatter myself they return my good will. At least appearances are to that effect. You have much at stake in the appearent coming events. You have your property and family. And your feelings from a long residence among the Californians may and should be interested in their favour. And what is their favour? Their patriotism points that they still belong to Mexico, but that feeling is continually leaving every one who has his farm and cattle to take care of, and will be but as a thing of other days, unless the supreem Government lends California a helping hand in good faith and for the actual good of the Inhabitants. As many beleive this will not happen, at least untill this generation has passed from the buisy scenes before us, they, often dispairing of seeing their own Statesmen come forward and save a sinking people, have and are looking abroad for succour and assistance. Some look to England, some to the United States and a few to France. The last is a "denier resort." Those who look to Europe know nothing of an English Colonist life or the heavy tax and impositions he suffers. The idea of Independence is from his Mothers breast implanted in every Native of the American Continent. Then where should he under imposition or a state of distrust look to for assistance? Only to the United States of America. He will there meet a fellow feeling, with those who can and will particapate in all his ideas & principles and hail him as a Republican and a citizen of the land of Freedom! Be all these things as they may, from the time of Mr Monroe, the United States have said that no Europian Government should plant colinies in North America. Mr Polk reiterates this assertion, and his Government will make it good. And the day that the Europian Colonists by purchase or the Europian Soldier by War places his foot on California Soil, that day shall we see the hardy sons of the West come to the rescue. I have thus given my opinions on the state of affairs in California to you as a freind and countryman of mine, and as a freind of California. As in saying I care not who hears you read this letter, I must insist on its not going out of your hands, nor of a Copy being taken *by any one*. You will oblige me by carefully reading it, and with the same care giving me an answer. As I know you have always prefered excitment to indolence, and a name and character to being one of the common herd, have been much in the political votex of California, I must ask of you, if you will inform me by a safe conveyance, from time to time, of any wish on the part of the Government or people your way to change or better their condition, should circumstances require it. I shall visit the south this summer.

I am Sir your most obt.
Thomas O. Larkin

I would send you Mexican papers, but those who rec'd them have sent them North. You will much oblige me by informing me why D. Pablo goes South.

[Larkin to Stearns, S. Coll.]

Monterey May 1, 1846

Mr Abel Stearns
Sir,

By Don Pablo de la Guerra two days back I sent to you four pages of writen matter on the principal topic of the day. Mr Henry Mellus, who is with me waiting for the Barnstable, advised me to send the letter by Captain Vincent, but believing Don Pablo honorable I sent by him that with his arrival you should have the news of the day. Should by chance this letter not arrive (I also sent two documents), by all means find out how it *miscarried* and hunt it up. Yet I believe Pablo will give it to you.

Knowing as you do the state of this country can not continue as it is, as [sic] should like to have your opinion of a change, and what your principal Neighbors think on the subject.

If there is war you know the result as far as regards this country. If the affair should be made up concerning Texas, the old claims Etc. and yet C. be left as it is, the subject of emmigration comes next. The result of this we may imagine. The officers of the Ship report as having seen in the papers at home of February (I had to near March and the 14 of M of Mexico) that 175 passingers *left* N.Y. by water in February with cargo for C., thence to the Origon—if the ports of the first were prepared for free cargoes—and that 1000 men were to start for the river or place called San Bernardino somewhere your way, Williams Rancho, I am here told. All this may or may not be. John Everett in Jan. writed to me that the Mormon waggons, so says the Newspapers of that day, would reach over 20 miles. In my own opinion, war brings by land thousands, U.S. Troops and Emmigrants. If peace, I presume the North will have an addition of a thousand people in October. Captain Hastings has left New Helvetia to meet them, tis said. The English have offered to leave the O. question to Nations or persons. Mr Polk will do nothing of the kind. Little by little he will give it up. Dr McLaughlin and all his Factors, officers & servants are now under the laws of the provincial Gov't of the Am at the Columbia, so Mr Mactavish, the new H. B. C. Agent now in Y. Buena informed me. He has orders to wind up, and sell the houses for 5000$. I believe Mr Forbes has been repremanded[10] by Mr Barron for mentioning political C. subjects in his letter. I think Mr Spence will receive the appointment. Mr S. dread an English Colony. He has no nead of Cradles nor wants Coffens but does not wish to see them and every thing else including sun shine taxed in California. Senors Castro, M Castro, Vallejo, Carrillo, Alvarado & Prudon are still here in Committee and have I suppose sent Don Pablo down to call up Don Pio. I hope he will come. It may be of much advan-

---

[10] Forbes was not reprimanded but was advised that the British government was not at that time anxious to secure new colonies. See Ephraim D. Adams, "English Interest in the Annexation of California," *American Historical Review*, XIV (1909), 744-763. James Alexander Forbes was a Scottish merchant who came to California in 1831. He was British vice-consul at Monterey, 1843-48. Spence did not replace Forbes, who remained in office until the vice-consulate was closed. Bancroft, III, 743.

tage to the country. He should also bring two or three of the Legislature. There is here no fear that the Gov. need have. He should have visited us last year. If its possible for you to leave home, it would afford me much satisfaction to see you at my house a few weeks while this committee are in session, and that you come with the Govr to Monterey or San Luis, should the latter come here for this session. I would willinging pay one hundred dollars towards your road expences for the satisfaction of seeing you here at present.

I shall proberbly write no more to you untill my first letter is answered, as I do not know whether you may fancy my stile of writing. As a merchant I wrote warmly & as a merchant, and to the purpose of my business. If I have changed or should change, I must still write or try to write to the purposes I follow.

Its possible, tho' in my opinion premature, that the Committee of Safety may think of declaring themselfs independent directly. One reason with the hope of contining so, the other that the squadron would not viset them in War as a part of Mexico. The difference in so short a time no Com^s would see. Prehaps the Comm^tte aim at San Luis for their meeting.

Yrs in hast

L

[Larkin to Leidesdorff, LE 130]

Monterey May 20, 1846

Captain William A. Leidesdorff
Yerba Buena
Sir

By the Courier now sent North, you will hear of the appointed Deputation or Junta that the Governor and Assembly have ordered to meet in Santa Barbara on the 15 of June next. Its object I know not. Prehaps the party concerned have no definet object in view, only expecting to realize some public benefit to the country. It is possible that they have some great affair on the tapis.

The "Portsmouth" waits the arrival of the Congress, then proceeds to your port unless something not anticipated prevents. The Congress' future movements I am not aware of, but suppose she will sail for Mazatlan and prehaps return direct to California again. Its impossible to say whether the war may take place. If it does not—and Mexico should not sell C—we shall for some years after 46, or 47, be in rather a disturbed state from the prevailing affairs of this country. I have not heard from Mr Gillispie since he left your house.

I am &c Yrs
Thomas O. Larkin

[Larkin to Leidesdorff, LE 131]

Monterey May 24 1846

Captain W. A. Leidesdorff
Sir.

I presume that the Portsmouth will leave here on the first of June for your Port. In case the Congress does not arrive by that time, the P. will remain in St. F. a few days or more, according to curcumstances. By her I expect to send your clothes.

By *private* conveyance I have rec'd an official letter from the Sub Prefecto, to your office, denying the right of Foreigners to hold land. From the paper it also appears that more was doing in your vicinity than elsewhere relative to Foreigners. An American has appeared before with a Frenchman to the Fr Consul complaining of being called away very often from their work by Sr Estudieno [Estudillo?]. I wondered you did not notify me of this affair respecting land. I am verbaly inform'd that some Bando or private conversation has been held respecting Foreigners not being able to collect amounts due for their wages when due. I will see the Senor Prefecto respecting the Sub Prefecto orders to you, and know why I was not informed of the curcumstances.

I believe that the whole state of this country will change in two or three years, yet it may not. And if my beleive proves correct, we may in the mean time have much trouble, disturbances, prehaps loss of property, even loss of lifes. Therefore we should be very gaurded in our actions and expressions.

Of my future letters do not have much to say, neither no words nor actions. Should any letter or person arrive, neither try to make much or little of the curcumstances, treating both as an affair of your daily rotine of business.

I rec'd some time back from Mr Dalton Bark 15 Salmon without advices, and could not tell even who sent them but tried to suppose Vincent, as they came from his ship, yet could not believe any person from a Boston Vessel could do so much. I then imagined you sent them.

Supposing this I gave the German Capt some, and others to different officers & [word undecipherable] People as your gift. I now find I am chg 18$ for 18 salmon. Hereafter plase send bills with any shipments. I do not understand this affair. I shall expect yr whole sale price for the Blue drill, not what I gave for it.

I will send you forms for making out Consular bills for board when I have time.

Yrs Respectfully
Thomas O. Larkin

[Swasey to Leidesdorff, LE 135]

Monterey May 28th 1846

W. A. Leidsdorff Esqr
Dear Sir.

I wish you would be so kind, as to forward my Trunk and Valise to me by the first opportunity, as I am very much in want of some of the things they contain.

I am now engaged with Mr Larkin to do his writing for him, and have been the most of the time I have been in Monterey. I do not know how long I shall stay with him, probably as long as I satisfy him. If you ever should have any business in Monterey while I am here, I should be very happy to do it for you, or any other way I can be of service to you.

The Ship Vandalia sails to day for the leward. Nothing new of importance stiring here, except the proposed meeting of the Governours. Mr Forbes is on board the Vandalia going to see the Governour to ask for land, *so he says*. Well it may that he is. Please present my respects to Capt Hinckley and Lady, Mrs Rea &c. The rest don't need any from me. Please direct my things to the care of Mr Larkin, and Oblige Your Obt. Sevt.

W. F. Swasey[11]

---

[11] William F. Swasey. Native of Maine. Came overland to California in 1845. Employed successively by Sutter, W. H. Davis, and Larkin. See Bancroft, V, 741, and Swasey, *The Early Days and Men of California*, pp. 9-47.

[Larkin to Leidesdorff, LE 136]

Monterey May 29/46

William A. Leidesdorff Esq
Sir—

Your letter with a mail Bag for the "Portsmouth" and another for several Person in and about Monterey, I rec'd this morning at seven, forwarded by Mr G. Thompson, for which I paid forty dollars. *Very high.* When you saw how well the mail was done up for the "Portsmouth" I wonder you did not do up the other the same. Excepting three or four lines from Mr H. Grimes, I found nothing for me. No mail, that you supposed of consequence, should leave you without being well done up, or a seald list of the letters you send. This Bag had but a piece of twine round it. How many people have handled it, or letters taken out, I can not tell, tho' I suppose none. But hereafter be very carefull about puting up a Foreign Mail, and who brings it. For want of such care, correspondence of the utmost importance may fall into wrong hands. By your Sub Prefect I sent to you a letter yesterday. Let me know if you rec'd it. Its non receipt would be disagreeable tho' not injurious. I suppose he would take care of your letters.

I am &c in hast yrs
Thomas O. Larkin

As you saw but one letter to me, you should have given me more news. I know nothing. The Portsmouth and Barnstable leave here on the 1 or 2d for your port. By the Purser Watmough, you will have your clothes. He will send by first Boat. I wish you to send to Captain Sutter to assist and forward to Monterey, post hast & by *proper hands,* any mail or letters that may reach his place for me, at my expence, if he think the importance warrents the expence.

[Larkin to Leidesdorff, LE 141]

Pueblo de San Jose
June 7—1846—

William A. Leidesdorff Esq
Sir.

When I dispatched Mr Neale[12] last Monday morning, altho' I had two men cop[y]ing, I could take no time to write to you. I understand

---

[12] Samuel Neal (or Neale). Arrived in California in 1844 (possibly also came earlier) with Frémont. Employed by Sutter. Guided Gillespie in 1846 up Sacramento Valley. Died in 1859. Bancroft, IV, 752.

that Neale arrived back by Sea to your place and continued up the River on the Sonoma side. I gave him two letters, the duplicates of each to remain in your hands, the others for him to carry direct to Lawson's [Lassen's] Rancho, which directions I supposed have been followed. I gave directions to Don Rafael Pinto[13] to take back your two Horses. Have you rec'd them. If not write to some one here to look them up.

This letter I deliver to Mr H. Mellus with the other enclosed to be delivered personally to you, which you will only deliver to the owner. You should receive this monday night. I shall wait here untill Wednesday morning at Nine to hear from you if you have any information worth sending, from Mr G.[14] I am anxious to hear from [you] by Tuesday or Wednesday morning. Was it not for fear of being recalled to Mont. by the arrival of one of our Ships of War, I would go to Yerba B. with Mr Mellus, but do not wish to be more than one days ride from home. I send to you the enclosed unsealed that you may know some of the news of the day, and to save my farther writing at present, which when read you will put immediately in an envelope, sealed up, and place it in your desk until Mr G arrives, should he not be already there. Should he be over the Bay, on bord the "Portmouth," I wish him to have it Monday night that he may answer it in time. The news of this place and St. Clara are nothing worth relating that I know of. Gen. Castro returned from Sonoma yesterday afternoon. He goes I believe to Santa Barbara.

I shall with some anxiety wait to see who and how many arrived in C. next October. I have wrote to Captain Sutter to send me a special messenger at the moment, and presume he will do so.

I am with respect
Your &c
Thomas O. Larkin

---

13 See Bancroft, IV, 780-781.
14 "Mr. G" is Archibald Gillespie.

[Larkin to Leidesdorff, LE 142]

Pueblo de San Jose June 8, 1846

Sir

With this I forward a letter for Mr A. H. G.[15] which you will retain untill he returns to your house. When I spoke of your lending the Boy Horses I alluded to the one you sent with the Officers. During the day I had to take the other, and ought to have said to you not to lend him any. But it all turn'd out right.

Respecting your Horses lend to Mr Neale, you will arainged with Mr G. but know from Mr Pinto where he left one, and send to some one here to look him up. Any Courier coming to me I must hereafter make good the horse flesh to you, if the Person who start the mail to you does not. I am purchasing 10 or 12 Horses, and the next Courier can leave your Horse in M. and take one of mine. The second can return the animal again. The Boy arrived here at 4 o'clock this afternoon, having left you this morning. I do not however approve of taking up any person this way to conduct correspondence. I am inclined to think the Junta is about giving up, and I may not go south untill the Congress arrives and I hear from Mazatlan.

I am your obt. Servant
Thomas O. Larkin

I am here to see the great guns
and big bugs, but have it under
stood that I am mining.
W. A. Leidesdorff Eq

[Larkin to Stearns, S. Coll.]

Sir—   Monterey June 14, 1846

The Congress can not be here before the 25 instant, judging from the time I know she left Calliao for Oahu. This will prevent me from being in Santa Barbara. Another reason is that I am well informed that the meeting will not convene as preposed. I feel very certain that your Neighbors have not rec'd the advice you mentioned to set up for them, the proposal [?] offering assistance. Yet I hope you will fully in-

---

[15] Archibald Gillespie.

form me on the subject. Have you seen Don Jose' letter to Don Pio relative to the proposed Junta. If strong is well, it is certainly well wrote, stringent if not deserving. I should not have anticipated a letter of the kind between the two under present curcumstances. I have the last few days been at the commandancia at Santa Clara. General Castro left the Pueblo with me on the 10 for this town. Sr Carrillo remains there. Various letters have over land reach'd several People in California from Men of Spirit, funds, activity, and some influence, who say they, with thousands, will be here in October. The emigration has begun and will proceed; good nor bad reports will not retard it. I have in print a long message of Gov Abernethy of Origon dated Decr 2, 1846 [1845]. It give the state of the country for the year, & is, I believe, of N.Y. The message was to their Legislature.

Altho' I suppose the Junta will not take place, yet the Assembly and the chosen members from the South may meet. Should this take place, and you imagine any request is to be made on any foreign Power in Eurupe, or they think of declaring themselfs independent, you will oblige me by informing me immediately. And should you think it of any benifet that I should be there, you can dispatch a Courier for me. In any case, if I can hear from Mazatlan of the War question being done away, or delayed, I may go to San Pedro in the Congress or the Portsmouth. I should not however choose to land from a ship of war at St. B. during the session. It would appear to imposing. I wish to move with less note and free of remarks.

My remarks to you or requests I make are under the idea that you are willing, nay anxious, to be once more *in* the U.S. There may be some of our Countrymen who do not have this wish. I presume by my letters you are not of this class. Should you be, please undeceive me before our correspondence is farther extended. I have not the least doubt but the fate of this Department wants but *one* or *two* years to show the world the way fate has predicted, and but few more to settle the question, even supposing Negociation nor war settles it not much sooner.

We have in Monterey the Rev Mr Macnamara[16] who arrived here from Mazatlan in H.B.M. Ship Juno. The officers of the ship where by the Captain prohibited from bringing letters. Mr M. is a chatolic Priest (an Irishman) has been in the City of Mexico all 1844. With Herrera, almost concluded a negociation for the London Emigation Society to

---

16 For a detailed and balanced account of the Eugene McNamara colonization scheme see Bancroft, V, 215-223.

land ten thousand Irish in C. Paredes refused to allowe any Emigrant whose native language was English, adding that the Irish in C. would join the yankees at once. Mr M. dresses in Citizens clothes, has in my opinion full as much government & political information as theological. He and the Captain of the "Juno" appear to be satisfied that no Government course can prevent the destiny of C. as it now appears to be going.

I have purchased a farm at Sonoma. I have repeatedly advised those in power in Monterey to ask for large tracts of land by which means they will become rich, as in a few years they may not stand as they do now, and all will find their level according to their merits. The Prefecto of this district, I believe, does not see affairs as I see them, and yet believes their usual fortune will carry them though. The Origon question remains as it was. Only the Government at W. [h]as given I understand the 12 mos notice to England. 8000 M. soldiers where on the banks of the River del Norte. 500 horse were to cross to see if Gen. Taylor (U S A) would oppose them. If he did, the 500 were to retire and the whole 8000 were [to] attack Taylor "se dice" and drive him. I suppose the line may yet begin at this river, run up to a parallel with the Gila River, then follow that due W. to the Red River just above the gulf of C, strike over, and enter the Pacific at or near the Bay of San Franc or mission of San Miguel [to?] some 30 leagues South of San Diego (will this embrace the copper mines of Don Juan Bandini).

Gen. Ynestro died in Mexico. 100,000$ could have be raised by his Gov't. He would not start under 300,000$. The [word undecipherable] I suppose is used up. The vessels have rec'd their false frieght and are discharged. Col. Tellas is said to be in Tepic. My Mazatlan Agent says the whole is explosed. Mr Macnamara has correspondence for the Bishop, now goes South, will call on the Gov. I suppose. He brought to me letters of reccommendation from our Consul in Mexico. He has a very good appearance. His actual business I presume to be of a private nature as Agent for his company to find available lands for the Irish. I should think his Government had cognizance of the business, prehaps affords assistance. Will you inform me of his motives and movements as far as they may come to your knowledge and anything else worthy of note. Did you rec'd several letters from me by Mr Forbes. There was one very important paper. No other person holds a copy.

I am your most
obedient
Thomas O. Larkin

Mr. Abel Stearns
Angeles—

[Larkin to Leidesdorff, LE 503(2)]

[Undated][17]

Since my last to you respecting sending up the River to see to the Courier, which you write you have done, I see by the papers of April that passed, Midshipman Woodworth (Capt. M.[18] will by this conveyance have the papers) was leaving St Louis for Indepence[19] to come to the Pacific with a mail. I presume the Mexican mails where supposed stopped or unsafe. You will therefore as a Merchant write again to Mr Bidwell and some other proper person to go up the river should they hear of any such Courier, and whenever met, have the person brought down in a Boat or the most safest way to you or Capt. M., charging to yourself or me the expence. By the same way I now forward this, you could send it, but the P.[20] would be best. But not by hand by any means. I know nothing about this Courier, why he should come or what information he may bring, yet wish to assist him. Should you be able to obtain drafts of 2, 3 or 4000$ from the same person who in M. gave me some and to the same person I suppose, I will give you some of the Angola's Cargo at fair prices. Take the drafts at the same rates you may take them in trade. Should you give cash for them at a discount, I will for the goods take them at par. I owe in Salem 4200$ and should like to have near that sum. In 15 days I may have an opportunity of sending one home. Altho' you may not have this amount at present in money, prosvisions and clothing, he could give you the draft and take up for his men as they may want. I presume his number of people will never be less than what he may want them for.

I know nothing about whether his former drafts were paid or not. Yet should he need any thing in my way, I hope he will command me.

[Unsigned]

---

[17] Reference to the *Angola's* cargo dates this letter as about mid-June 1846.
[18] Captain John Berrien Montgomery.
[19] Independence, Mo.
[20] The U.S.S. *Portsmouth.*

V. The Bear Flag—"The Taking of Sonoma"

June-July 1846

THE Bear Flag Revolt and the proclamation of a "California Republic" at Sonoma by a party of Americans who took the town on June 14 and sent General Vallejo and others as prisoners to Sutter's Fort came as a complete surprise to Larkin and upset all his plans, for Vallejo had been the most pro-American of the California leaders at the junta in Monterey two months earlier. Meanwhile the Santa Barbara meeting had been abandoned by Pico, who had never been enthusiastic about it and who was more in favor of seeking British than American protection, though he took no positive step in this direction until after hearing about the capture of Sonoma.

In an atmosphere of mounting excitement and tension, Larkin first received "Verbal Information" and then, later the same day (June 18), letters from both Leidesdorff and Montgomery describing the Bear Flag outbreak. These letters have been previously published, but Larkin's first reactions to them and to the news they contained are here printed for the first time. His primary concern seems to have been to prevent injury to innocent persons, and his next to obtain more accurate and detailed information to incorporate in his dispatches to the State Department and in his letters to Stearns and his other friends further removed than he was from the center of disturbance. Forbes, the British vice-consul, relayed to him (on June 26) some very wild rumors that showed how ill-informed *he* was, and Sutter, who had been forced by Frémont to harbor Vallejo and his fellow prisoners at Fort Helvetia and to give up its control to Edward Kern, was hardly informative, but importunate as always, two days later. No wonder then that as late as July 1 Larkin had still to confess that "The Northern affair is beyond my comprehension." By July 5 he thought that "We are now geting the truth," and he was already revising his earlier opinion that Frémont and Gillespie had not been involved in any way in the planning of the Bear movement. Without knowing that Frémont had already reached Sonoma and assumed command of the "California Volunteers" there (on June 25), Larkin rightly surmised that the movement was growing in size and momentum daily. He expected it to spread to Monterey "in 15 or 20 days." There was some talk among the Spanish Californians there of taking Larkin into custody and holding him as a hostage to ensure good treatment and a speedy release for Vallejo. His fellow Americans, fearing for his safety, organized a posse to protect him, but Larkin himself did not at this time show any great alarm.

Stearns, at the safe distance of Los Angeles, was still more concerned with business than with politics and was seeking (on July 3) to arrange to supply beef to the British squadron that was soon to arrive in the wake of Commodore John D. Sloat's ships, which had reached Monterey on July 2.

[Larkin to Stearns, S. Coll.]

Monterey June 18th 1846

Sir

Verbal Information reached the Yerba Buena (by the Sonoma Alcalde who left in a hurry, from thence forwarded Officially by the Sub Prefect to the General) that last week Sixty Foreigners took Sonoma, made prisenors of, and carried off M. G. Vallijo, Salvador Vallijo, Victor Pruden and J. P. Leese and all the Horses. They committed no other excesses, and left twenty five men in charge of the place.

The week before Don Francisco Arce with twelve men were passing the Sacramento River, near Sutters. While at Martin Murphy House eating breakfast outside of the house round their camp fire, they receive a visit from twelve Foreigners who took of the corall about one hundred and seventy Horses and mares belonging to the Government, leaving the Soldiers their saddled Horses and each a horse extra. They then departed.

Although this news has created considerable excitement here, yet (I beleive) no one has any fears respecting the result. It is said that the Foreigners have taken posession of Captain Sutter's Fort. I have no writen information of these affairs, and can give no opinion. I merely give the news as I have received them.

I Remain Your
Obedient Servent,
Thomas O. Larkin

Abel Stearns Esq
Angeles—

[Larkin to Leidesdorff, LE 149]

Monterey June 18 1846

Captain W. A. Leidesdorff
Dear Sir

I last week forwarded to Mr Weber under cover to you a letter to Captain Montgomery, and one not sealed to Mr G. I understood Mr W. himself put them on board the Launch. Did you receive them. They contained information of the Mexican and American Troops on the Rio Norte, also saying to Capt M. that he prehaps would meet the "Congress" here about the 26th as she was to leave Callio for Oahu the first week in April, and on the 17 of May was supposed to be off Hilo. I am aware that Don Jose had the Rio del Norte News as from my letters and thought they might have mislaid.

Now more than ever we must know who carries our letters. I am supprised that you did not informed me at the moment respecting the taking of Sonoma, and carring off Messrs Prudon, Leese & the two Vallejo by Foreigners. I can hardly believe it and do not understand the affair, altho' in the Pueblo and in M. I am supposed to be well acquanted with the whole. Do not hereafter let such important news passed unnoticed.

Last week, while I was at the North, arrived here Am Barque Angola (of Salem Mass) Saml Varney. She has lately been trading and selling Cargo at the Islands. Came here to sell the residue. How the Captain could expect I do not know. He on arrival wished to enter part of his cargo, sell and leave. This Don Pablo would not allow. On my arrival the latter allowed me a day to see if I could purchase the cargo, otherwise the Bark would leave. Don P. said the vessel must enter like all others, but I could make my own trade with the Gen. which I did, payable a little in cash, the remaineded half goods (which I gave at Mr Mellus' prices) half Government debts, on overhauling the goods. (The vessel was searched first, opening draws, trunks & pockets where they found 23 ps silk hffs, a private affair and adventure of the Capt or Mate). The C.H. was shut up and the delivery of goods refused me. I saw the fact in the eyes of the Senors a minute before. On going up Stairs my only answer was Veremos, which I refused to take. I found out the contract in writing between the Gen & me was to be declared null. Next day I demanded my goods. No. My list of duties. No, not untill I would come forward and promise to follow the orders of the A^d and present myself and two securities, should I have the list. I told Don P. I owed nothing untill I saw the a/c and no Securities could be obtained untill they saw the amt, that I must see Don Jose first, that the goods or half of them where sufficent, to all which he said no importa. Rising up, said I, I only am chief here and the Gen. and all other should know it. That untill I confessed Etc., promised Etc., and signed the bond to pay him, the list should not be made out. On leaving the office I told him it would be a pleasure to me to compromise with him, if he would meet me half way. But no, that day he and, I think, Mr H concluded to refuse to make out the list and say the vessel's cargo was not to be enter'd, that I should be published as a smuggler of a whole cargo, that they would retire. I on my part was willing to accept Don Rafael, Jacinto, Beneto or Charves for my administrador. It was supposed next day that those who choose to leave the C.H. must also leave this district. Yesterday before breakfast Don Pablo requested my presence at 10 at his office where I found him and all others remarkable pleasant. The goods are *to day* in *my* ware house and over 17000$ paid (whole amt 18000$ and over) of the duties ballance will be to day.* A final courier from the General will reach here to day, but I now do not need him.

I have the largest lot of wide & narrow Mantas, white and brown, Blue drill, Blue Manta & Callicoes that was ever landed in this town, also Iron, loaf sugar and fancy cane seat chairs. And should like to sell you 3 to 4000$ cheap and on time. The Mantas are 28 to 36 inches. Drill and Blue Manta & the Callicos very good. You can name your prices and the amnt and will answer you.

Yrs in hast
Thomas O. Larkin

Over 100 Bales & Cases, [the word "has" crossed out] 2/3 paid for.
*[*In the margin:* not one rial or vara to the C.H.]

[Larkin to Leidesdorff, LE 150]

Monterey June 18 1846
Thursday Night 10 o clock

William M. [A.] Leidesdorff
Sir

Your letter and the Captain's[1] came this moment to hand. The Boy wishes to return immediately on account of his Horses—and being taken himself—as I have no news to give in return, I dispatch him. From Mr Stokes you will have a letter of mine wrote this morning.

I am very thankfull you wrote, tho' the most of my information came from the Captain's letter. The cause deserved a Courier. You will send again when you think it best to do so. Send word to Stokes or Mr Weber to purchase two good horses and keep them in Mr W. drove subject to your order. They will do for a change. Prehaps I will send two by yr next Courier.

I dont doubt but Capt H.[2] is all you write, but its all to no purpose. Let him go on. There is no remedy. Nor do I care whether the officers are one thing or another, its not my affair. Capt. M. gave me much information—what and who was at work. All this he picked up by chance. Do by all means keep me informed of the state of affairs. Your two letters come in good time as this night I was for the Maria Terese making up my dispatch[3] by hear say for Washington. Therefore am very glad you and Capt M. wrote.

Of course there is some excitement here. People left town to day under Joaquin Escarmia. More go tomorrow under the Prefecto & Sor Alvarado. To me in person all appear very pleasant and treat me well. There will not many leave here for the North. There is a suppossition that this affair is started by Fremont and G. and that I was aware of it. I knew nothing and dont believe they do.[4] I supposed it was a personal affair. It now appears laid out with form. I hope the four persons taken will be well used. To say I hope it will stop is of no use. If they have started the big Ball to roll forever and thro & thro' C, I can not stop it.

---

[1] Captain Montgomery. His letter is printed by Hammond, V, 35-36, as is Leidesdorff's of June 17, in V, 36-38.

[2] Captain Hinckley.

[3] This dispatch addressed to Secretary of State Buchanan and dated June 18 and June 19, 1846, is printed by Hammond, V, 41-44.

[4] Larkin was to revise this opinion very soon.

Its very late, and I have wrote all day. I will write you agan soon. Again thankfull to you & Capt M for yr letters.

I am &c

Thomas O. Larkin

Show this to Capt M.
Can you not get Foreign Couriers?

[Larkin to Leidesdorff, LE 503(1)]

[Undated][5]

In the affair going on, I wish you to charge the principals to have every care taken that from want of thought, hurry, ignorance of the character of the person they meet, from temper of there adherents, from former privates piques or enmity, that no innocent person shall be injured, that the people's persons nor feelings shall be troubled where they are peacable attending to there own proper affairs—this, I hope, the principals will duly charge their men to see to. I suppose Horses for the Saddle & Bullocks for food will be taken. Even then it should [be] carefully done. By this means the Natives will become contented and their own party will receive additions. I do not mention this supposing the cheufs think other wise, still I wish to mention it.

Again, great care should be taken that no Subjects of other Nation should be compelled to come out for or againt the party. Let them alone. They are coming without any extra exertion. Force may call the attentions of some English Naval Captain take [sic] seak out his countryman and injure the party. We understand that Murphy, Bale, Went, Janes, Black & Ridley are prisoners. I think its not so . . . [end of page—rest missing].

[Larkin to Stearns and Temple, S. Coll.]

Monterey 22 June 46

Gentlemen—

By a private conveyance sent to Senors Diaz, Abrego, Spence and myself this morning we rec'd the following,[6] which was found put up

---

5 This undated fragment of a letter, undoubtedly written during the second half of June 1846, is included because of its significant reference to the Bear Flag revolution and its possible consequences.

6 There is no enclosure, but the reference is undoubtedly to Ide's second proclamation, dated June 18, 1846, and since printed in many books dealing with California (as in Hammond, V, 53-54).

at the Pueblo de San Jose the 21 instant. Gen. Castro has not as yet give us this information.

From information this week I find that Mr Ide arrived at the Sacremento riv last year, has a wife and five children, about 45 yrs of age, a well informed, active, and stering person, was once a Mormon preacher (he said), left them, no longer agreeing with the sec or party. 'Tis suppose he expects a party in July from the Origon, and several in Sept from the States.

The Portsmouth is at San Franci, the Cyane here. The Salem Bark Angola, Samuel Varney, lately touched here to try the market. I purchased the whole cargo, 100 & odd Bales & Boxes, Domistic & Prints, some rice, Sugar & Iron. Duties $18,250$ exclusive of tonage, all paid, and two thirds of the Invoice to the Capt. If you want any Brown Mantas, 28 to 36 inches wide at market prices, payable in 1847, send me word and you have them.

I am yours &c
Thomas O. Larkin

Messrs
Abel Stearns &
John Temple

[*On back of letter:* There are many suppose if I have to do with the late rise. I know nothing of it, or its people, and shall prehaps be the last person they speak to on the Subject. We hear that their flag is a White Union, red fly and a Star & a Bear in the Union.]

[James Alexander Forbes to Stearns, S. Coll.]

St Pedro 26th June 46

Abel Stearns, Esqr
My Dear Sir

The Juno arrived here yesterday the 25th and will leave here this day for Sta Barbara and St. Franci.

I must refer you to Mr. Howard for the news from Mexico.

It appears that the foreigners at the north, learning that Castro, under pretence of attacking Capt Fremonts party, received 100 horses in purchase from Vallejo, but having obtained intelligence that Castro intended to attack the Govt., gathered a small party, and falling upon the party conducting those horses, took them all: after which they the same party of foreigners, seized upon the two Vallejos, Mr. Lease and Prudon, and made prisoners of them, probably with the intention of delivering them up to Govr Pico.[7]

It is therefore easy to account for the non appearance of Castro in your quarter, and it appears very evident that the foreigners at the north are animated by the same sentiments as those of the south.

Capt Blake informs me that it is the intention of D. Pio to proceed to the north and annihilate the party of Castro, who has left Monterey, at war with D. Pablo Noriega, on account of some arbitrary measures of Castro respecting the payment of duties of the ship Angola. D. Pablo has shut up the Custom House.

Please inform Mr. Workman and others of the Contents of this.

I hope Mr. Workman will join D. Pio and place himself at the head of the foreigners to aid in the pacification of this Dept.

I am My Dear Sir,
Yours sincerely,
J. Alex. Forbes

[Sutter to Leidesdorff, LE 155]

New Helvetia 28th June 1846.

Wm A. Leidesdorff Esqre
Dear Sir!

As all Comunication between here and the bay is suspended, except the Man of War boats, I wish you would do me the favour to send me a small supply of Brandy or Aguardte and some Sugar by the first Opportunity, as I have a good many visitors, officers of the Man of War and other Gentlemen, likewise some Gentlemen prisoners which I wanted to treat so well as possible.

I am now in great want of bags. You remember that Mr Zarembo, vice Govr, told me in your presence that I could get the loan of a part of the bags left in your charge. If you could send them likewise by a man of war boat you would oblige me very much, and no doubt every Officer who visits this place will do me the favour to bring me these necessary articles up here. The bags I need to bring the Wheat from the Aera's [?] in the Magasins and to send it down in the Launch, as I cannot send the Wheat in bulk before the Launch can be repaired.

---

7 Forbes's confused picture of the situation indicates the amount of rumor and speculation that had arisen.

A few pieces of Manta and good Cotton thread likewise a few other articles like Callico, Hdkfs. etc., if you have them on hand, would accomodate me very much. Seven man from the Oregon Company arrived here the day before yesterday in a hurry to join our forces, all of them about 200 persons (150 men which carry Arms) will be here in about 10 days.

The Emigrants from the U. States will be here this time in the Month of August, because Capt. Hastings is gone so far as fort Pritcher [Bridger] to bring them a new route discovered by Capt frémont which is about 3-400 miles shorter as the old route over fort Hall. The foreigners will be very strong this fall. Lieutt Rivière can give you all the news of the place.

I remain very respectfully

Your

Most Obedient Servant

Jn. A. Sutter

P.S. Please have the Goodness
to forward the inclosed
letters by Opportunity's.

P.S. The new Comers from Oregon say when the Hudsons bay Compy Ship bring the News of this Revolution to Oregon that certain about 200 young Men would be bound for here to arrive this fall. We are nearly out again with writing paper and letter paper.

[Sutter to Leidesdorff, LE 157]

New Helvetia 1th July 1846

Wm A. Leidesdorff Esqre
Dear Sir!

In my last letter I forgott to write you for some tumblers. I wish you would be so good to send me 1 or 1 1/2 dozen of them. Sugar I have only for a few days more, and my house is just like a great Hotel. I have to board the Garrison, the Gentlemen and comun prisoners, 13 in all. The Garrison is from 20 to 25 white Men. Beside this a many visitors are coming and going. The Man of War boat will take for me what you will have the Goodness to send me up by her.

I hope that I can send the Launch in a very short time. When you send me some Manta and print, please send me 1 lb. of good Cotton thread.

So soon as the Launch can go below I will send you the Indians.
I remain very respectfully

Your
Obedient Servant
Jn. A. Sutter

[Larkin to Leidesdorff, LE 158]

Monterey July 1, 1846

William A. Leidesdorff Esq
U. S. Vice Consul
Sir

I have just dispatched a letter to Mr Weber for you, supposing it might from the Pueblo find an early conveyance to you. If its lost, its of not much consequence.

We are exceedingly in the dark respecting the news from the War party. Last Sunday, 4 days back, news by express from General Castro and some letters reached us—that Captain de la Torre's party were attacked by the opposite party who fired their rifles on them without effect and then turned and run, that de la Torre and party gave pursuit and in the chase ordered Baptise Castro to return to the Gen. with the news, Baptise having lanced 2 or 3, his party having killed several and was killing the remained, that from some pistol shots fired backward the Natives lost three men. The truth of this we can not decide on. I do not credit it. There are other reports here making out a great slaughter among the Countrymen. This is, however, contradicted. Messrs Spence, Diaz, Abrego and myself send up Rose to day to learn the particulars. By him and Don Antonio Osio I rec'd your letters and am much obliged to you. They were much saught after here.

By Moscow's clerk, Mr Richardson, I sent to you a letter that I hope you have rec'd. Inform me.

I suppose the Portsmouth or Cyane will remain at your port for a time, prehaps both. You will have more Ships of War and Whale Ships this year than ever and do a very good cash business by November. I should suppose you could not purchase too many provissions for them. Will not the disturbances hurt the trade, prevent killing of Cattle and attending to the fields. As affairs are now, they assuredly will.

Should Captain Philps intend to stop here going down and will let you have any of my goods (excepting chairs of which I have no more),

I will give him the same here and he will much oblige me. Should he not, you will receive them per first opportunity.

My situation is such that I do not want any article of Merchandize on hand. I purchased the Cargo to please the General and the Angola's Captain more than any thing else. I shall therefore dispose of it at once, that I may be free to leave Monterey any day I choose, leaving only a large Capital that Mr Green rec'd in January. You will oblige me much by working off as many as possible. Send me all news you can, but nothing of a compromising nature by land. The Northern affair is beyond my comprehension. Therefore I must not commit myself or you in the business. Are you aware I was invited last week to go to Santa Clara to see the General, and offered to go, on receiving the invitation in writing in certain forms—that I named from the proper authorities, which I did not receivve. When Don Jose A. Carrillo came here with 15 soldiers to inforce against the Adm my "Angola" Contract with Don Jose Castro, Don Pablo had give in—during their remain here. Carrillo and another proposed making me Prisoner. By the warm persuadesions of Don Alvarado and Jimeno he gave it up. Another party would like to make me a Prisoner, to urge on the squadron to seize the Country and settle the business at once. They may yet take me as a reprisal or offsett to the Senor Vallejo, according to how the war goes at Sonoma or the Sacremento. In the mean time tongues are lively in particular females ones. I think Mrs Hartnell's sister rather carry the palm or have found a new Dictionary. Prehaps the former is on the stand. Mr Hartnell has made up his mind that the Ide party is extinguished before this. I do not care whether I am made Prisoner or not providing I sleap in a good Bed, under cover, and have tea or coffee before I start in the morning and during the day. They for the rest may furnish Beans and Tortillas if they like. I have taken an account of debts and property and am pretty well prepared for any thing. As you are not yet recognized, they will not trouble you. My respects to the officers.

I am yours respectifully
Thomas O. Larkin

[Stearns to Johnson, S. Coll.]

Angeles July 3ᵈ 1846

Mr James Johnson
Dear Sir—

I rec'd yours of the first inst. in which you observe there is a prospect of some English men of war arriving. I hope it may be the Case and that they may want a plenty of beef and that you may have the Chance of Supplying them.

Should they arrive, you can always have from me from four to five hundred large novillos of four to five years old, which for beef would be the most advantageous. Make the best bargain you can and all over a fair price for such Cattle will be for yourself. Perhaps the best way would be to treat for a certain price the quintal, as John bull would understand that way of trading best and then large Cattle would count up, Say from two to three dollars a quintal, or such price as you might think best for to make something out of the job in case there is a chance. Good fat weathers I would furnish you at fourteen reales and have a plenty of them.

The Cattle could be delivered at the shortest notice.

If you have a chance, try and make something out of it. John Bull is a lusty old fellow and has a stiff purse.

Bills would be the same as Cash. With many expresions to the ladies and I remain yours &c

A. S.

[Larkin to Leidesdorff, LE 159]

Monterey July 5 1846

Sir

I am very sorry not to have rec'd a letter from you by Mr Harrison,[8] and suppose you did not know of his leaving for this place. We are now geting the truth of the different curcumstances that have happened your way. Certainly the Bear goes ahead beyond all Animals in these

---

[8] Napoleon B. Harrison, midshipman on the U.S.S. *Portsmouth*. Sent by Montgomery to Sloat with dispatches. Bancroft, III, 777.

parts. Should not be supprised to see him here in 15 or 20 days. If he does come, I suppose he will enter, as people do not seem enclined to prevent him. The enclosed are without superscription or direction for reasons you will understand. Altho' I do not doubt the safety of the conveyance still they may fail. Write often. And anticipate a good year for trade.

I am yours &
Thomas O Larkin

I do not know when the
other Vessels go up. Suppose
one or more will soon.

VI. The American Occupation— Army versus Navy

July 1846-May 1847

On July 7, 1846, Commodore Sloat ran up the Stars and Stripes over the customhouse at Monterey and in a proclamation that Larkin helped to draft (though he had pleaded that this action should be delayed for two or three weeks) announced an American occupation of California. Sloat met with no resistance. On July 9 the American flag also flew over San Francisco and Sonoma, and the "California Republic" was no more. Frémont and his "Volunteers" (now made honest men by being sworn into the service of the United States) left Sonoma to march to Monterey, where they were received coldly by both Sloat and Larkin but excited the interest and admiration of the officers of Admiral Sir George F. Seymour's *Collingwood*, which had meanwhile arrived there.

Larkin, feeling that Othello's occupation was gone and having many unsettled claims on the United States government, as well as much that he wished to report verbally to his superiors, wanted to "proceed immediately" to Washington, but Commodore Sloat prevented his departure. Larkin told Leidesdorff that there was no prospect of any new office for either of them, but in fact the State Department soon requested Larkin to continue to act as its confidential agent, and the Navy Department also offered him employment. This invitation was not extended to Leidesdorff, who now concentrated once more on his trading and hotel-keeping activities at Yerba Buena. His appointment as vice-consul there had never in fact been officially approved by the State Department or accepted by the Mexican government, though he had functioned as such for nearly nine months.

Commodore Robert F. Stockton, who succeeded Sloat, sent Larkin down to Los Angeles to help in the pacification of the southern areas of

84

Alta California, but, owing to the failure of Stearns and other leading American Angelenos to give Larkin the co-operation he asked of them, his visit was somewhat frustrating. He was back again in Monterey by September, "out of office and Government employ" and a few hundred dollars the poorer. A great many trading and personal debts were owing to him and proving hard to collect. It appears that the free-spending Lieutenant Gillespie also owed money to Leidesdorff and was seeking to repudiate that debt. Then came Larkin's one exposure to real danger, his capture, toward the end of 1846, by Californians who were still re-sisting the American occupation, and his imprisonment in Los Angeles, which was again in the hands of the patriots. Though at first threatened with summary execution, he was on the whole treated very well and was fed copiously. His wife, evacuated to San Francisco (as Yerba Buena was now officially called), fared less well, and his youngest daughter, Adeline, died there of a fever during Larkin's imprisonment. By February 1847 he was home once more, safe and sound, and was soon planning to leave Monterey for good and to locate himself in San Francisco, which was starting to boom. He already had extensive real estate interests there, and the following year he went to San Francisco permanently.

A crisis in the military government of California had followed the recapture of Los Angeles by the patriots. General Kearny decided to take back Colonel Frémont (whom Commodore Stockton had appointed military governor) to the United States under open arrest, there to accuse him of insubordination and to have him court-martialed. Frémont, who had carefully cultivated the more important among the American settlers in California and who had commissioned Larkin to purchase an estate for him near Santa Cruz, left with Abel Stearns's very interesting and revealing letter of May 23, 1847, in his pocket. The fear of "all good Citizens" that California might be returned to Mexico under the terms of a treaty of peace was also for a time shared by Larkin.

[Larkin to Leidesdorff, LE 163]

Monterey July 16, 1846[1]

W. A. Leidesdorff Esq
Sir.

Yours of the 12 instant I have received. I can not with propriety at

---

[1] Reply to letter from Leidesdorff printed in Hammond, V, 130-131.

present seak for any office for you, and do not intend to for myself. You took office not for profet, for fame and character only, which it has given it. It leaves you in a more desireable situation than you could have enjoyed had you not accepted it. As to the expence, I suppose you allude to house keeping, that thro' taste and hospitalty you have had and will have thro' choose and generosity. The times will bring all forward who have talents and make all rich who have as much industry and activety as you have.

I do not know what to request of you respecting purchasing land for me, not having any available funds on hand. By Mr Davis' Brig, now two days sailed, I sent to you over 3000$ worth of goods, and by land last week advised you, which letter, with one for Purser Watmough from his Brother, was taken from the Courier by Manuel Castro, 2ᵈ (chanata), and carried to Santa Barbara as a prize. The letters of importance were not found. They were brot back and since sent to Capt M. by Mr Stokes. Some of these goods I sent by your order. The others I wish you would sell at such prices as you can on a year credit taken Notes, with interest after that date. I wish to be free from all trade, having a desire to proceed immediatley for Washington, all tho' I may not, Comʳ Sloat not being willing that I should leave him. I am anxious to go to assist in carring out what has been begun. As by no manner of means should affairs now change. Should by any future convention in 1847 the flag be changed, it would not be Mexican again long, as the Bear would rise in his strengh treble in /47 to what we have seen in /46.

You can therefore take all I send, and dispose of them soon as possible as the prices you may think they are worth, but not under the idea that goods will fall in 1846.

I in a former letter, which came back, enclosed your paid Note. (It is erased and chancelled). I will again send it. The Congress, Comʳ Stockton, arrived yesterday direct from Oahu. No news. I dont know her number of days passage. Take care of the enclosed letter for Sen Prudon.[2]

I am yours &c
Thomas O Larkin

---

2 The Prudon letter is not in the Leidesdorff manuscripts, nor is it printed in Hammond; but a letter from Colonel Victor Prudon to Larkin, dated July 23, 1846, and printed in Hammond, V, 156-158, in Spanish with English translation, refers to Larkin's "gratifying letter of the 16th inst." He writes from the "Prison of the Sacramento."

[Larkin to Leidesdorff, LE 184]

Monterey September 21/46

Dear Sir

After spending a few weeks and a few hundred dollars in bringing about the grand issue, I am at home again.[3] We both may now consider ourselfs out of office and Government employ. Still we have not lost but gained. Commerce will revive. In fact, all and every one may now flourish in California. You from your houses, house lots, farm and commerce must become rich. Its my wish, that once being connected with you in office, to point out to you some future prospects more than others enjoy, but do not known that I can. Time will unfold to you all advantages, and you will depend on me in any available case within my power.

Messrs Howard and Mellus have forwarded orders to their clerks to prepare their house for the Com[r] who leaves here on thursday for your port. I have mentioned to the Com[r] that prehaps he might like your house. At any rate, that you would feel a pleasure in attending to him. You could also oblige him by having three good saddle Horses for himself and staff—one in particular for himself.

If your house[4] is in good order, you might pay an early visit on board and say to Com[r] Stockton that you have rooms for him. He will want two or three apart from others, having his own Cooks and Stewards, that he can live private or receive company. You will find him a frank, brave and open hearted Gentleman.

I expect to be at your house within 10 or 12 days and shall depend on a room in your house, in case the Com[r] does not occupy to many. You can, if you choose, in your first visit to him say I have requested you to offer your services to him.

I am yours &c &c
Thomas O. Larkin

William A. Leidesdorff Esq
    Y. Buena

Private I have purchased the two or three leagues of land at point Lobos to near your town and shall ask your assistance in taking care of it. Do not pretend to know this.

---

[3] From Los Angeles.
[4] Presumably the City Hotel, on Portsmouth Square (the old Plaza), owned by Leidesdorff.

[Larkin to Leidesdorff, LE 185a]

Monterey Sept 22 1846

William A. Leidesdorff

Sir

By your letter to Mr Green, I find you have paid Mr Gillispie $416/— four hundred and sixteen dollars. I have asked Mr G. sometime back how much he rec'd from you. His answerd, I owe him nothing, having all ways had cash. I made have misunderstood him. At any rate it matters not as I have near that sum of his or to his order on which he is drawing.

Your Note of Mr Grimes is near or quite 800$ with interest, I claiming on the whole amount, you on settlement with me claiming interest on Capt Gillespie. I have drawn on you this day in favor of Don Carlos Rousillon[5] for four hundred dollars, which please pay at sight, and the difference, for or against you, we will settle next week. Should you be without a part of the 400$, ask Mr Davis in my name to advance.

I am yours
Thomas O. Larkin

[Larkin to Leidesdorff, LE 231]

Monterey 11 Feb. 1847

Capt. W. A. Leidesdorff

Dear Sir

I am happy to inform you I am again at home. I've had, as you may imagine, some ups and downs. Twice aimed at to be shot, once by a man in anger in an action, once by a drunkard at the Pueblo. I was closely confined, more so than the others, but had never less than 4 or 5 meals sent to me a day, 4 or 5 courses each meal. Shirts, Stockings, Hkfs. &c, even money offered me by Flores. The Mexicans & C. appeared desires to out do each other in obtaining my good will. The last ten days I was at Don Luis's Vinyard, where at last there was 15 or 20 famili[es] who came for Protection there. I had no gaurds. Had I felt like it, I had much fair company to converse with. Misses Adalaide &

---

5 Charles Roussillon (or Rossignon), French trader. Came to California in 1843 (or even possibly in 1837 or 1833). Living in Santa Cruz in 1846. Bancroft, V, 705.

Anna Johnstone[6] among other fellow Prisoners. As I was liable to be marched for Mexico each day, I was poor Company.

With this you have some Newspapers up to 29 Aug 46.

You will please accept my sincere and warmest thanks for your kind and constant attentions to Mrs Larkin during her distressing times in Yerba Buena, and present the same to Mrs Eager[7] and her two Daughters, Mary and Arabilla. Say to them to hereafter command my friendship and services as they please. Give my thanks to Mr Howard and Mr Bartlett[8] for their kind assistance to my Wife. How much care and trouble could have been saved to Mrs Larkin and our children, had Mr Mellus been disposed towards us in house room, as he and every Agent (in my time) of his Employers has found me in Mont. When I first applyed to him for his house, he said it would incomode Jos. Thompson. The latter had prepared me to waive his claim. Mr M. then said he must consult Mr Howard, when he should arrive, as he might dislike my taking their house. I told him I knew H. better than that. Had Mrs Larkin had a house to herself, I believe my favourite child would now be with me.[9] At any rate, much inconvenence and crying moments would have been spared my Wife.

I should suppose Mr Brown[10] and his wife had less feeling than the chairs they occupied. I believe Mrs B. did not enter my child' sick room untill it was dead. Then Mrs L. was advised not to accept any services from her. Mr Reading wishes you to fence in his lot by the Middle of April. I want you in my name to occupy that water lot in front of my Vallejo lot. Put some loads of Stone on it and fence on board in the two sides. Please do this quick and suddenly.

Your obet
Thomas O. Larkin

We will do something in the
trade way by & by your way.

---

6 Misses Adelaide and Anita Johnson. Adelaide and Anita were two of the three daughters of James Johnson, English trader who came to California in 1833-34. These two married Francis and Henry Mellus, respectively. Bancroft, IV, 693.

7 Mrs. Lucy E. Eagar, mother of John Eagar, a member of Brannan's Mormon party. Eagar came to Yerba Buena with his mother, his brother, and two sisters in 1846. Was Brannan's clerk and also associate editor of the *California Star* newspaper. Bancroft, II, 787.

8 Lieutenant Washington A. Bartlett, U.S.N. First American alcalde of San Francisco, 1846-47. Bancroft, II, 712.

9 Larkin's youngest daughter, Adeline, died in San Francisco in 1846.

10 Probably John Henry Brown, English sailor and San Francisco bartender and hotel keeper, who married Hetty C. Pell in December 1846 and in April 1847 advertised her as having left him. Bancroft, II, 732-733.

[Frémont to Stearns, S. Coll.]

Camp on the Salinas river near Monterey,
May 19, 1847.

My dear Sir,

I send you this note by Jacob, whom business requires me to send to your city. I regret that I have not my affairs sufficiently arranged to write you on matters of business by so certain a conveyance, but I will endeavor to find another equally so before I leave. I was disappointed not to see you before but hope that no unpleasant accident detained you at the rancho. On some subjects of general importance to the country I should have been to have had your views and did wrong to postpone informing myself to so late an hour. I might have been useful at home. When you reply to this which I trust you will not fail to do by Jacob, I will thank you to mention any one particular thing or measure which may occur to you as useful here at this time.

Nothing of interest is going on here, so far as is known to me. Every thing and every body appear quiet, the only busy people are the horse thieves. I am told that one of the rancheros sent in word that they had heard of a new governor and would like to see some of his men. Even the newspaper formerly published here has been removed to Yerba Buena. Mr. Larkin is there at present and I suppose will soon locate himself there.

I have commenced my preparations for the homeward march and in about a week shall be ready to start.

Commodore Biddle goes home in the Columbus immediately after the departure of our party. Commodore Shubrick will remain in command. He had been sent to capture Guaymas, Mazatlan and Acapulco, and the Preble has been sent to bring him back. Please present my remembrances to the family.

I am with much respect and regard
Your obedt Servt,
J. C. Frémont.

[Stearns to Frémont, S. Coll.]

Angl. May 23, 1847.

Charles T. [John C.] Fremont, Esqr.
Dear Sir—

By your servt. Jacob I rec'd this morning yours of the 19th inst. I regret not to have seen you the morning before you left as I had intended; my delay was caused by some difficulties which took place between the Servants and which I had to settle. I arrived in the morning, a short time after you left. Have the Publishers of the "Californian" taken fright that they have moved from Monterey to San Franco, or do they wish to pass the warm season in the fog of the latter place?

As you are about to leave this "Western Star" for the more brillant ones of the east, it is to be supposed you will communicate immediately with the Govt. or heads of department and from your acquired knowledge of the affairs and people of this [word "Department" crossed out] *not little* important Territory, you will use your influence to Secure to California what is *most desired* by all good Citizens, both native and foreign residents: 1st, that this may never be returned to Mexico, 2d, that the Goverment of the U.S. will, as soon as posible, establish a permanent territorial govt. with a wise and select council named by the goverment itself, 3d as the judiciary department of Califa is in a bad state, or I may say we have none at all, that the govt. of the territory be empowered to appoint all the necessary officers to this most impor[tant] branch of all goverments, 4th, and not least, procure to send a number of Catholick Clergymen who understand the Castillian Language, men of liberal principles and good moral character. Such men would be of much importance, both to the govt. and welfare of the people, 5th, Should Califa ultimately compose a part of the U.S., a govt. armed steamer would be of importance to ply between this and Panama, as probably at present the most prompt means of facilitating the interests and communications of the govt. and people its master.

6th, Should war continue with Mexico, some additional force of regular troops should be sent here.

I have thought proper to note the above observations which perhaps might serve you as a memorandum to remind you a little of the place you are to leave, and its necesities.

You will undoubtedly inform some of your friends (Merchants in the States) that there is a Scarcity of goods in Califa of every discription. Some well assorted Cargoes would return the merchant a sure profit. Dry goods, groceries, Hard, Crockery & Glass ware, furniture, Boots, Shoes, Hats, &cr all are wanted.

[Unsigned]

VII. Gold from the American River— but Not for the Late Mr. Leidesdorff

September 1847 - October 1848

PICKING up the threads of his commercial affairs after the interlude of his brush with history, Larkin sought to settle outstanding matters with Leidesdorff, but the two fell out during the autumn of 1847 over Leidesdorff's bill, and the latter very sharply broke off business relations with Larkin on October 14. They appear to have had very little to do with each other during the seven months that Leidesdorff still had to live. It was the unhappy end of a very fruitful association.

The news of the discovery of gold at Sutter's Mill on the American River was at first communicated by the "Lord of New Helvetia" only to a few close friends and business associates, among whom was Leidesdorff, who had let him have large quantities of goods on credit and to whom Sutter must have owed a large bill at the time. The offer of a share in a company to exploit the gold discoveries was made within two months of James Marshall's first find in the millrace, but Sutter was still very cautious about the extent of the deposits. Sutter's close associate Pierson B. Reading, who was farming in the upper Sacramento Valley and who was one of the substantial Americans there who (like John Bidwell) had not participated in the Bear Flag affair, undertook to investigate the gold-mining possibilities of Leidesdorff's own property on the upper Sacramento. He obtained the help of James Marshall himself for the modest fee (in the circumstances) of $25.00, and their report to Leidesdorff was very encouraging. This must have been one of the very last letters Leidesdorff received before his short and fatal illness in May 1848.

The letter of ex-British Vice-Consul Forbes, who was now preparing to become a loyal American, could not have been read by Leidesdorff, for it is dated May 15, 1848, the day on which he died. It is typical of Forbes's muddleheaded opportunism, which had led him in the past to invite rebukes both from Lord Aberdeen and from Lord Palmerston and which caused him so completely to misunderstand the nature of the Bear Flag Revolt. The "person" he was prepared to recommend was in all probability himself. Forbes was already active in exploiting the quicksilver mines at New Almaden near San Jose where he resided, and he did have some knowledge of minerals. His letter indicates that the news of the gold discoveries was getting around, though it was not until June 1848 that their extent began to be realized in San Francisco or that the real gold rush commenced. Benjamin R. Buckelew, who made and engraved a silver coffin plate for the late William A. Leidesdorff, was one of the first to advertise that he would buy gold, in the columns of the two San Francisco newspapers, of one of which he was for a time the publisher. The papers had to suspend publication in July owing to the departure of their printers—and most of their readers—for the mines.

The news of gold took much longer to reach the East, and its importance was not fully realized there until the gold discoveries were mentioned in President Polk's annual message at the end of the year, but Gillespie's letter of October 15 to Stearns, from New York, indicates that the news was already causing excitement there by that date.

[Larkin to Leidesdorff, LE 331]

Monterey 21 Sept. 47

Captain W. A. Leidesdorff

It is some time since I heard from you. I have before this requested my account in full from you, but did not obtain it.

I some time back understood it was supposed in your town that I did not wish to sell the lot I advertise. I really do. I want funds to build. Having sent so much home, I am now short. Tell me what you think the 60 ft front worth.

In addition to my office of Navy Agent, I am now appointed Navy Store Keeper. I hope it will not cause me too much trouble. I suppose there will be a Seperate Person in six months to this office. I've sufficen[t].

Yrs in hast
Larkin

[Larkin to Leidesdorff, LE 337]

Monterey Oct 10/47

Capt. W A. Leidesdorff
Drsr

I have your letter and account before me. The account is entirely wrong and not drawn from your Ledger as I ever saw it. The last of October we were square. A large bill you now insert of Lt Gillispie is paid. Altho' you had no unlimited order to advance to him for me, I paid you in cash and rec'd from him a draft, to say no more on the subject with you. Several charges you now add, relative to the funeral of my child. Mrs Larkin paid you. Courier to Monterey I paid you, and sent on your rec'pt 216$ to Mr West. I told you I had nothing to do with. When he and I made a contract I paid him the amt due. Don Benito debt I informed you was not good. Castarneda I pay, yet think I did not receive it. My want of care is not your loss in this case. 150$ in boards I think was not delivered. The fencing of the two Lots for Mr Green and myself, I do not want, much less the fencing the Forbes lot. When I was with you, I said at the expiration of one year, if these two Lots were worth the money, I would ask for them again, but did not want any expence occured on them. Neither Mr Green or my self can accept the fencing or pay any expence on these lots. Even if you worked for our safety, next year would have answered.

I supposed the Governor would have made your house his home while in S.F. When I told him I had wrote to you to prepard I thought it pleased him. Prehaps others did not want him with you.

I see the Council think of overhauling old a/cs. I think they can not annul any old contract, altho' they may say it was not for the benifet of your town.

The Preble sails to day for Panama, passinger Captain J. B. Hull,[1] Dr Powell[2] & Mr Wilson.[3]

Yrs &

Thomas O. Larkin

---

[1] Captain Joseph B. Hull, commander of the U.S.S. *Warren*, 1843-47. Bancroft, III, 791.

[2] Dr. William J. Powell, surgeon on the U.S.S. *Warren*. Powell Street, San Francisco, was probably named after him. Bancroft, IV, 783.

[3] Henry Wilson, purser of the U.S.S. *Preble* in 1847. Bancroft, V, 777.

[Sutter to Leidesdorff, LE 413]

New Helvetia March 25th 1848

Wm A. Leidesdorff Esqre
Dear Sir!

The launch "Dicemi Nana" arrived here on the 17th instt evening. My Wagons has all been in the Mountains then, and I thought it would be the best to send her up to my farm "Hock," as the house is right on the river banck. I furnished the Canaea's imediately with a good pilot and crew to take them up, likewise plenty of provisions.

We has had last Sunday, and several other day's in this week, very bad stormy weather, that they had to lay by, and one day they lost themselves in company with their countrymen. I furnish them again with provision, for which I charge nothing. The Launch have 180 fanegas of Wheat. To complet the 1500 fanegas for the Russians, I have to send 416 1/2 fanegas more.

My Launch has not arrived yet, but I hope she will be in the river.

My Sawmill in the Mountains is now completed. She cuts 2000 feet of planks in 12 hour's. The Grist mill is advancing.

We intend to form a company for working the Gold mines, which prove to be very rich. Would you not take a share in it? So soon as if it would not pay well, we could stop it at any time.

I have the honnor to be

Your
Obedient Servant
J A Sutter

[Reading to Leidesdorff, LE 426]

New Helvetia April 29th 1848

Captn W. A. Leidesdorff
My Dear Sir

Enclosed please find a letter from Col J. C. Fremont to your address, also one for Mr Abel Stearns and another for Mr John Roland, which please have the goodness to forward by first opportunity. I also send to your care a letter for Major Snyder who is residing at Santa Cruz.

Some more recent discoveries on the upper part of your ranch prove that the gold washing could be pursued with much profit.

Tomorrow I shall leave for the upper part of the Valley. On my return will write you the news.

> I am, Very truly
> Your Obdt Svt.
> P. B. Reading

[Reading to Leidesdorff, LE 427]

New Helvetia April 29th/48[4]

Captn W. A. Leidesdorff
My Dear Sir

Yesterday I returned from my trip to the Mountains, and after carefully examining that part of your ranch which extends into the hills, have the pleasure to anounce to you that it covers a part of the great "Placaro." Gold has been found within ten miles of your house, and I am certain that it is still nearer. I do not write from mere conjecture, but from facts which I have proven. I am sorry to have detained your Launch so long, but it was impossible to have made a careful examination in less time. Your Mayo Domo I did not call on for horses, or any assistance whatever.

As the gold region on your land covers the whole of the Eastern part of the ranch and is a "Placaro," I have not of course made any denouncement.

After Searching for two days in the hills, I found the Mormon Camp, which I beleive to be about 16 miles from your house. They are washing on the South fork of the American Fork, about 1 1/2 miles from the junction of the North and South forks. As you did not inform me how far your lines run East from you[r] house, I did not feel at liberty to take the responsibilty to order them off. In a few days, say 6 or 7, I shall leave for my ranch and shall not return to this place under Six weeks.

Should you come up or send any person as your agent, the first gold washing will be found in the first Creek, Say 10 Miles from your house, and on the river, it will be found about two miles nearer. There is no person at work, neither has there been within about 16 miles and there the Mormons only, about 15 in number.

I was obliged to take Mr James W. Marshall with Me in exploring

---

4 This letter must have been misdated by Reading, as it refers to events several days subsequent to April 29 (the date of the previous letter to Leidesdorff).

your land, for which I agread as your agent to pay him Twenty five Dollars. He was with me three days, leaving the Saw Mill and two Placero's which he is working. I could not get him for less. This is the only expense attending my trip, and I am happy to have had it in my power to render you my Services.

As Regards the Barley and Corn, Mr Dutton had not deposited it at Hock, not having received my letter in time. It would have detained the Launch too long for him to have hauled it, the roads being in some places very bad.

Mr Marshall is Much in want of some articles which I enumerate on the Enclosed Slip. The am't over the 25$ which is due him, as before mentioned, he will pay you in *gold* from the "Placero" which he is working. I will write you again on my return from above. Please send up the articles for Marshall by the first oppor'ty, mark^d in his name.

Yours truly
Reading

[James Alexander Forbes to Leidesdorff, LE 428]

Santa Clara 15th May 1848

My Dear Sir

I have heard a great deal about your gold washings, and have this morning been informed that there is really a great quantity of gold upon your land. If you feel disposed to secure to yourself the profit to be derived from this important discovery, I can reccommend to you a person who will be happy to enter into an agreement with you for the washing of the earth containing the gold and to attend to its collection.

I have been expecting to see you up here for some days past in relation to your mining prospects.

If I can be of any service to you, please inform me by first opportunity, and at all events, if you desire the services of a person who has great Knowledge of minerals and the practical operation of their benefice, and whom I can reccommend as a strictly honest and respectable person.

I am My dear Sir
Yours Sincerely
Jas Alex Forbes

[Buckelew to Leidesdorff Estate, LE 432]

San Francisco
May 18, 1848

Estate of Wm A. Leidesdorff

To B. R. Buckelew, Dr.

May 18th	To Furnishing Sheet Silver for Coffin plate for deceased	$2.00
	To preparing & Engraving the same	6.00
	amt Recd 18th July	$8.00

B R Buckelew[5]

[Gillespie to Stearns, S. Coll.]

New York October 15th 1848

My Dear Sir.

Your kind letter dated 1st May came to hand on the 1st of August last. I was then at Washington, still waiting upon Congress, and the quickness and despatch of the Express was the subject of admiration & comment of every person. Carson, indeed, won new applause, and upon his arrival he was greeted by many friends.

I was very happy to hear from you, and am very much surprised and astonished that you did not hear from me; for from Napa Valley, I sent a packet to San Francisco with a letter for you, in which I gave you the reasons why funds could not be procured, and assuring you that I would not lose sight of the interests of those who had been so kind to me. This promise I have faithfully kept, and but for the opposition of the Whigs, and the enemies of Col Benton, I would now be in California, with means of paying all claims. I say the Enemies of Col Benton because the Bill for the payment of California Claims, having been bro't forward by him, and the name of Col Fremont having been put in the Bill, as one of the Commissioners, it passed the Senate after a hard

---

5 Buckelew advertised in the *Californian* newspaper on May 24 and 29, 1848, "GOLD! GOLD!! GOLD!! Cash will be paid for California Gold by B. R. BUCKELEW, Watch Maker and Jeweller, San Francisco." He had reached California overland in 1846 and settled in San Francisco. For a time he was publisher of the *Californian*. He died in 1859 at the age of 37. Bancroft, II, 734.

struggle, and laid over in the house, altogether in consequence of a desire to oppose them, and to show that they (the members of the Military Committee of the House) would not favor any measure with which they were connected; and besides, Col Mason & Col Stevenson sent letters to the Department of War, setting forth some of the transactions of Col Fremont in the South, as having been entirely of a private nature, and making it appear that he intended to defraud the Government. These persons in this but followed out the pitiful course they had begun, to endeavor to injure those who had labored in the country, where they came but to enjoy comfort and ease. The Bill after having been three months and a half before the Military Committee of the House, was reported one week before the adjournment of the Session, and is now amongst the first business for the coming winter; and I hope, that on or before the 1st of April, to be upon my way to the land of promise, to convince my friends that I do not forget them. I shall start for Washington this week, where I shall remain during the winter, in attendance upon Congress until our Bill has passed, and will use every means and every exertion to obtain its early passage. Every person in California to whom I am indebted, either in a public or private capacity, shall be fully satisfied, & nothing but circumstances beyond my control has delayed the payment until this time.

Col Fremont has left for the West. He is probably about starting from Westport for Santa Fé, from thence he will cross to California. He has fitted out an Expedition from private resources, and intends to make a full survey of the Country, and to publish a work to meet its expenses. He has with him many of his old party, all of whom are very desirous of returning to California. I presume Capt Hensley[6] has returned, or rather has arrived. He left the Frontiers in May and should now be in California. He was in Washington nearly all winter, and should you meet him he will be able to give you a full account of our affairs in this quarter. He left under the expectation of being one of the Commissioners for the Settlement of the Claims, but his name, like Fremont's, assisted to defeat the passage of the Bill last winter. It was very plainly seen that Fremont had made up a little family party, which did not suit the judgement of disinterested persons. It was generally understood that I was to have been one of the Commissioners, but I have

---

[6] Samuel J. Hensley. Came to California in 1843 as a trapper. Naturalized in 1844. Employed by Sutter and associated with the Bear Flag affair. Captain and later major in the California battalion in the south. Testified at Frémont's court martial. Resided at San Jose and died in 1866. Bancroft, III, 781.

been informed I was considered too independent & not sufficiently agreeable, consequently was left out. I am now very happy, as it has turned out, for there is no extra emolument, and I shall return to California under any circumstances. It is said, Mrs. Fremont accompanied by her Father will visit California in the Spring.

A considerable force to garrison California & Oregon is preparing to leave this by way of Cape Horn—One Regiment of Infantry, Three Companies of Dragoons, & two Companies of Artillery for California— Three Companies of Artillery for Oregon. Major General Persifer F. Smith is to Command both Territories. He takes with him a full staff and the Reg^t & Companies are fully officered. Many of the officers are married, and they all take their families with them. I am told, that there are upwards of fifty females with the command, some twenty-five or thirty very agreeable & interesting ladies. They go out in Three Steam Propellers and three sailing vessels. Brigadier Gen'l Riley is also in the Command. A Board has also been ordered to the Coast of California & Oregon for the purpose of locating LightHouses, Fortifications & Navy Yards. It is composed of Scientific men of the Engineers and Navy. Several Engineers are ordered with the Troops to remain permanently in the Country. Indeed, everything is being done which the interest and great importance of the Country demands.

The public in general are mad about California, & the late news respecting El placer has made many adventurers look towards that region. But there are very many solid people about to emigrate to California. There are several vessels to sail in all this month for San Diego & the ports to the North loaded with merchandise. The trade with that country has fairly opened, and you can now look for a regular supply of almost every thing you may desire. The Emigration next Spring overland will be very large, many families have already rendesvouz'd upon the frontier. The first Steamer has sailed for Rio de Janiero & Cape Horn to take her place in the line at Panama upon 1st January next. The California is a fine vessel & is one of three which will shorten the communication to thirty, if not to twenty-five days. The Panama is to sail upon the 1st November for the Pacific, and the Oregon will follow in a short time. The owners have put the price of passage at a very exorbitant rate, which will prevent many from traveling that way, but it will be reduced in a short time. They now charge $350 which is just $150 over what it should be.

The Presidential Election is now occupying public attention. There are three Candidates in the field, Cass, Taylor & Van Buren, the last the

Nigger Candidate. That is, he has set up the Free Soil party to defeat Gen'l Cass. Mr Van Buren expected the nomination in the place of Mr Cass, and not getting it, was so enraged, that under the pretext of opposing slavery he has come out a Free Soil man. The Election will be a very close one. Already have some of the State Elections taken place, and the vote been nearly equal. Ohio has elected a democratic Governor, whilst Penn^a has elected a Whig, but in this last State the feeling was purely local and cannot affect the general vote. The Whigs are rather blue, and some of them even go so far as to give up all chance of Gen'l Taylor's being elected. My impression is that Cass will be the President, and I am very sure I wish it, if for no other reason, than that he will take care of our beautiful California.

California will no doubt get a Government next winter. The Election being over, there will not be so much debate upon the Slave Question, and I doubt not but the Missouri Compromise line will be run to the Pacific. Slavery will never exist in California, and the question has been agitated solely for party purposes. Every exertion was made last winter to have a bill passed making a Government for that Territory, but the Whigs were determined not to grant it.

This will be carried to California by Mr Frank Ward,[7] who goes out with his Bride, a highly accomplished and agreeable lady, whom he married some ten days since. Mr. Ward intends now to reside permanently at San Francisco, and will no doubt carry on an extensive business. He is well informed on all matters relative to our affairs in this quarter, and will convey to those interested a true and correct account of the exact position of affairs.

Please present my best compliments to Mrs Stearns, as also, my best regards to Don Juan Bandini and his family. None of them have been forgotten. Memorias to all enquiring friends.

I had ne'er forgotten to inform you that your accounts, as well as those of all other claimants which I took with me to Monterey, are now deposited in an Iron Chest in Washington, waiting the action of Congress. I brought them with me by accident, and have so secured them that you cannot by any means meet with loss under any circumstances. They will return with me in April.

---

7 Frank Ward. Came to California in 1846 on ship *Brooklyn*. Opened a store in San Francisco. Returned east in 1848 but came back to California with his wife, Henrietta Zimmerman, who died in San Francisco in 1849. Went east again in 1853 but once more returned to California soon after 1870. Drowned himself some years later, according to Bancroft, V, 766-767.

Reiterating that I shall use my best endeavors to obtain an early settlement of all Claims, & hoping this will find you in the best health
I am

Very truly Your

M^t obt Servt.

Arch H. Gillespie

Abel Stearns Esqr
Los Angeles
   California.

Epilogue: A Decade Later—Halcyon Days No More

April-July 1856

WITH the discovery of gold in California and the beginning of the gold rush, a new era began in that once pastoral land that was to transform it out of all knowledge within a few years and to populate its cities and valleys and hills within a very short time. Larkin was a man of the pastoral stage in California's history, who, although he lived until 1858 and prospered mightily in the gold era and the days of the vigilantes (referred to in his letter of May 31, 1856), was never really at home in the new California.

His wistful remark in his letter to Stearns of April 24, 1856 (almost exactly ten years after he had received his appointment as United States confidential agent in California and eight years after he had given up his consular office), refers to the pastoral stage, in a rare burst of eloquence, as "Halcyon days," as indeed they had been for him. His nostalgia for those days caused him soon afterward to perform a labor of love for which all historians of California should feel greatly in his debt. He drew up a list of about three hundred names of United States citizens and British subjects who had lived in Upper California prior to 1840 and circulated this list, for correction and amplification, to other California pioneers. His intention to publish the list in the press was apparently not carried out, but his manuscript of it has been preserved in several copies, the most complete of which is reproduced as the Appendix to this volume.

[Larkin to Stearns, S. Coll.]

San Francisco, April 24" 1856

Abel Stearns Esq.
Dear Sir

I have to thank you for your kind and prompt attention to my last letter. Any case that I might have in the U.S. District Court in Los Angeles I should expect to place in charge of Mr Scott. The case I wrote to you about may or may not be mine to attend to in that court. I can not tell at present. In the meantime I thought it best to inquire if it had been appealed and what Attorney's name was on record in that Court, and if not appealed have it done and let it remain for the present. Enclosed[1] please find a copy of the paper you forwarded, for you to refer to. From the first part of it I should think the Claimant had appealed within the six months. By the last part of the Document it appears that the appeal was just taken by me. Please inform me if the Claimant (and when) took the appeal within the proper time. Will you ask Mr. Scott what his fee will amount to—to take charge of the case. Have it submitted and attend to it untill the final decision in that court in case I have this business to attend to, for myself, not for others.

I often have enquiries made from Persons living on your Mission Delores land, or from Persons having an interest there, how you are progressing in the affair. A Mr Hoff, who has a large House there & says he has spoken to you on the subject, appears to have a desire to see you or know how you progress in the case. I believe he expects to purchase from you, supposing your title will be fully confirmed to you. How do you Southrners like the Settlers Bill. De la Guerra, Wilson & Brent battled the Bill hard and manfully. Times are hard here—becoming harder—I begin to yearn after the times prior to July 1846 and all their honest pleasures and the flesh pots of those days. Halcyon days they were. *We* shall not enjoy there like again.

I am yours truly
Thomas O. Larkin

---

[1] There is no enclosed paper with the letter in the Stearns Collection.

[Larkin to Stearns, S. Coll.]

[*Written in corner:*
  Answered June 4ᵗʰ]

San Francisco May 31ˢᵗ 1856

Abel Stearns Esq
Dear Sir

I have yours of the 7 inst. to thank you for. On the arrival of your favor here, I was travelling in the mining country. While among the miners I heard of the shooting of Mr King.[2] I was in 3 or 4 localities as the news reached the people—such an excitement, such friendship, shown for one man, I never saw or heard of before. I such [saw] the People fill a Hotel as the stage gave out an Extra. A man would jump on the counter, read it aloud, then another person would read it to the crowd. The day King died, had the country been telagraphed for People to come to San F., the Steam Boats could not have carried them all. If for no other reason, I wish Mr King could have recovered to have known how high he stood in the opinion of the miners. The church was very full. During the funeral exercises I think I never saw so many men sheding tears at one time, the women universally. The procession was about one mile long. Every window & house top that we passed was crowded with people. And they say there was thousands at the same time to see the hanging. I heard of this hanging while in the procession. Casys funeral had 750 to 800 people. I saw *every* face (encluding some 50 females), and know *one* person by name & *two* by face. I expected to see some of the high friends of C. & some Gentlemen who are often on Montgomery St. in attendance, but did not one, but heard there was three of them. Our whole town yet remain in excitement in feeling. The "Committee" have 4 or 5 men in confinement. I suppose they will ship them. The U. S. courts have not stopt nor will they, nor need the State courts in town. One has because the judge has gone to Sonoma sick, the other because the judge has gone East and the judge who was to take his place is up country. Yet 'tis said that the Committee interfere—not a bit. In Kearney & Montgomery St. there is much talk for & against the Committee. In Sansome, Battery, Front Street, the Merchants are most of them members of the Committee. There never was in an association of 3000 men more inteligence, respect-

---

[2] James King of William, founder and editor of the San Francisco *Daily Evening Bulletin*. His murder by James P. Casey inspired the formation in 1856 of the Second Committee of Vigilance. Bancroft, IV, 700-701.

abiluty & wealth than in this one.[3] I mention this merely to show you who compose the "Mob." I suppose most of the small lawyers & the Pol[it]icians and all the loafers & gamblers are against the "Mob." 9/10 of those who I am personally acquainted with, and our Mechanics & Merchants generally, & half the best Lawyer, approve of the proceedings of the Committee. The first class expect that the Governor will be here to night and issue out a proclamation. If he does, I suppose it will, a la mode de Micheltoreno [be] a strong one.

I began this letter to speak of employing Mr Scott. I do not like to give 500$ for merely submitting the case in the district court and more money if there is much to be done. The charge in this District court is 100 to 500$— 600$ to 1000$—to take a case before this court & obtain the final confirmation in Washington. You will *know* in a month that 19/20 of the cases are not to be appealed to the Supreme Court. As I have all summer to attend to this case & write to Mr Scott before your judge arrives, there is no hurry. Chavis owned the grant and placed it in Limintour[4] hands to attend too. Both parties were away & the case was not attended to. I hold a Grantor's deed from Chavis for the land, and wish to offer a part of the land to an attorney to attend to it. Mr. Hoff was aware you intended to prosecute your Delores claim throu' both courts. He asked for information about purchasing before he put up more buildings or sold out. I forward you a pamplet respecting the late events. Are you coming *this* way this year.

Yours truly in hast
Larkin

---

3 This expression of sympathy and admiration for the Second Committee of Vigilance, which numbered among its members many of Larkin's friends, rather contradicts Underhill's impression (*From Cowhides to Golden Fleece*, p. 263) that Larkin disapproved of its actions.

4 Joseph Yves Limantour, French trader who came from Mexico to California in the *Ayacucho*, which was wrecked near Point Reyes. Opened a store in Yerba Buena. Supported Governor Micheltorena and obtained from him large grants of land, which he later sought to extend by means of forged documents before the land commission. The courts eventually rejected these. Bancroft, IV, 714.

[Larkin to Stearns, Den, and Spence, S. Coll.]

San Francisco June 14" 1856

Messrs Abel Stearns
  Nicholas Den[5]
  David Spence[6]
Gentlemen—

I am anxious through the public prints to perpetuate the names of all the English and American Residents in Alta California in 1834. With this you have the list as far as [I] have been able to make it out. Some less number of names can be found south of Monterey. Will you from your commercial Books, and from memory fill out the list as far as you can, and forward to me by the Second Steamer after you receive this letter. For fear of loss will you please duplicate by the following Steamer. Can you suggest any mode to perfect the plan I am carring out. Soon as I have the list printed I will forward to you the Newspaper, the "Chronicle."

       I am respectifully
       Thomas O. Larkin

Abel Stearns Esq

[Larkin to Stearns, Den, Wilson, Forbes, Cooper, and McElroy, S. Coll.]

San Francisco July 1st 1856

Messrs. Abel Stearns
  Nicholas A. Den
  John Wilson
  Jas. A. Forbes
  Jn. B. R. Cooper
  J. McElroy, Editor of "Pacific Sentinel"

Gentlemen.

I am endeavoring to obtain, for the purpose of perpetuating the information in the public prints, the names of all citizens of the United

---

5 Nicholas A. Den, Irish physician who came to California in 1836 and settled in Santa Barbara. Bancroft, II, 779.

6 A similar letter, addressed to David Spence alone, is in the Larkin documents in the Bancroft Library, dated June 15, 1856 (Vol. IX, No. 480).

States & British subjects who lived in Upper California prior to the year 1840, with the time of their arrival in the country, their professions, & the District in which they resided. I think that by referring to your old books, & by the aid of your memory, a very nearly perfect list can be made. It would be desirable to include in it also the names of the French & German residents, but I presume they were too sparsely settled through the country to render it practicable to obtain the particulars aright for, & therefore I have not attempted it.

From my own memory, aided by my old books, I have, as you see, made out a list comprising nearly 200 names. With the assistance of those I have called on, I presume we shall be able to add about 150 more. I have made six copies of my list & sent one to each of the gentlemen addressed above. Will you please retain the paper two or three weeks to enable you to consult other old residents in your vicinity, & when you have made all the additions & corrections, in spelling the names or in any other particulars which you may be able to, return the same to me. When I have received all the copies, I will carefully collate them, & have the list published with the names alphabetically arranged. I shall be happy to send you some copies if you desire it.[7] Hoping you will consider this a labor of love in which you will be pleased to write with me I am

Very respectfully
Your Obt. Svt.
Thomas O. Larkin

---

7 The Huntington Library has facsimile copies of two lists compiled by Larkin. The first (Fac. 35) is twenty pages, pp. 1-8 containing a list of 278 unalphabetized names and pp. 9-20 containing 236 alphabetized names. The second list (Fac. 36) contains 285 alphabetized names and is reproduced as an appendix to this work. The originals of these lists are in the possession of Collis Holladay and his sister Mrs. Helen H. Ord, of San Marino, California, who kindly permitted them to be inspected and collated with the copies. Another copy (HM 19961 in the Huntington Library) of the original list, containing 249 names and a slightly different preamble, was previously in the possession of Henry R. Wagner.

APPENDIX

The following list, Huntington Library Facsimile 36, from the original owned by Collis Holladay and Mrs. Helen H. Ord, was compiled by Thomas Oliver Larkin in July and August 1856. The list contains 285 names, of which 162 are identified as American, 60 as English, 21 as Irish, and 15 as Scotch, leaving the origins of the rest unidentified. A number of these names do not appear in Bancroft's "Pioneer Register." The name of "Jedidiah Smith" has been repeated, and there are numerous misspelled names, such as "Peter Lawson" for "Peter Lassen." The list is not comprehensive and, notably, omits the names of several of the men who went with Sutter to Fort Helvetia in 1839 or joined him there later.

NAMES OF THE BRITISH SUBJECTS, AND CITIZENS OF THE UNITED STATES WHO RESIDED IN ALTA CALIFORNIA—*prior to 1840—with their place of residence—profession and the year of their arrival. As far as can now be ascertained, during this period, there were living in California, a few French, Germans, Portuguese & Ita [lians] (not forty) and 30 to 40 Natives of the Sandwich Islands, and Foreigners of Color. Subjects of Spain and Citizens of the South American Republics were not classed as Foreigners.*

Married in California Marked M
Now living marked L
Dead marked D
Left Cal. Marked G

Persons Names	What Nation	Year of Arrival	Where Residing	Trade or Occupation	Married etc.
Allen George	I	1822	Monterey	Writer & School Master	M D
Anderson William	E		Santa Cruz	Lumberman	M L
Alezander David	I		Los Angeles	Merchant	L.
Alezander Cyrus					
Anderson Stephen	S	1826	Ship board	Ship owner & Supercargo	L. G.
Atherton F D	A	1836		Clerk	Married in Chile

Persons Names	What Nation	Year of Arrival	Where Residing	Trade or Occupation	Married in California Marked M / Now living marked L / Dead marked D / Left Cal. Marked G
Burke James	I	1824	Santa Barbara	Sea Otter Hunter & trading	M. L.
Burton John	A	1828	San Jose	Town Officer & Retailer	M. D.
Brown Charles	A	1829	San Francisco	Lumberman	M. L.
Burton Luis T.	A	1831	Santa Barbara	Sea Otter Hunter	M. L .
Branch Joseph	A	1831	Santa Barbara	Sea Otter Hunter	M. L.
Burroughs James	A				
Berry James	E		San Francisco	Officer, Mexican Army	D
Bowls Joseph	A		Monterey	Retailer	M. L.
Barker Robert S	A		do	Carpenter	G.
Breck William	A		San Luis	Gunsmith	D
Bale Edward T.	E	1839	Napa	Physician & Ranchero	M. D.
Bourn Thomas G.	A		San Jose	Retailer	M. D.
Bell Alezander	A	40	Los Angeles	Merchant Tailor	M. L.
Black James	E		Pajaro	Lumberman & Ranchero	M. L.
Banks Archabald	S		Monterey	Carpenter	G —
Byrns Edward	E		do	Teamster	
Byrns John	E		do	L.	
Bee Henry	E		do	Teamster	M. L.
Burton Joseph			do	Laborer	
Bennet Gerald	A				
Brown John	A				
Burroughs William	A				
Brander William	E		Monterey	Lumberman	
Bennet William	A				
Burns John	I	1823	San Luis Obispo	Laborer	D
Bullon Joseph					
Burton Herald					
Beidler Jonas		1836		Tailor	
Chapman George or Joseph	E	1818	Santa Barbara	Carpenter	M. D.
Cooper John B. R.	A	1823	Monterey	Sea Captain & Ranchero	M. L.
Cooper John	E	1828	do	Soldier, Mexican Army	M. L.
Call Daniel	A	1818	Santa Barbara	Carpenter	

Persons Names	What Nation	Year of Arrival	Where Residing	Trade or Occupation	Married in California Marked M / Now living marked L / Dead marked D / Left Cal. Marked G
Carpenter Lemuel	A	33	Los Angeles	Vinyard	
Coppenger John	I		Las Pulgas	Lumberman	M. D.
Cooper	A		Santa Barbara	Sea Otter Hunter, circus actor, Show man	D
Cooper David	E		San Francisco	Retailer	D.
Coulter Thomas		1834	Traveling	Naturalist	G
Chard William	A	1836	Santa Cruz	Lumberman & Trader	M. L.
Carmichial Laurence	S		Monterey	Retailer	D. Killed
Cole Thomas	E		do	Teamster & Herdsman	M. L.
Chappel George	E		Santa Cruz	Lumberman	M. D.
Clar John	A	1836	San Francisco	Engineer	L.
Collens Peter	A				
Cooke James	E			L	
Campbell Colin	A				
Campbell Samuel			Mont.	Lumberman	
Chamberlain John	A		Monterey	Blacksmith	L.
Cooper Marten					
Doak Thomas	A	1818	Monterey	Carpenter	M. L.
Duckworth Walter	E	1822	do	Teamster & Gardner	M. D.
Dana William G.	A	1824	Santa Barbara	Merchant & Ranchero	M. L.
Douglas David	S	1831	Traveling	Botanist	D.
Dye Job F.	A	1832	Monterey	Merchant & Ranchero	M. L.
Day Benjamin	A		do	Hatter	G
Day William	A		Los Angeles	Hatter	G
Davis John C.	E		San Francisco	Shipwright & trading	M D
Davis John C. Mrs.	A		do		M. D.
Dickey William	I	1826	Sacramento	Disteller	G
Den Nicholas A.	I		Santa Barbara	Physician, & Ranchero	M. L.
Daly Nathan	A		Monterey	Disteller	D.
Daylor William	A				
Domingo John	A				
Dolieron Manuel	A				
Dun		1836		Hatter	

Persons Names	What Nation	Year of Arrival	Where Residing	Trade or Occupation	Married in California Marked M; Now living marked L; Dead marked D; Left Cal. Marked G
Elwell Robert	A	1824	Santa Barbara	Merchant	M. L.
Ebbets John	A	1832	Monterey	Importer	L G
Everett John	A	1832	Los Angeles	Supercargo	L G
Estabrock Ethan	A		Monterey		L
Edmands Nathan	A		"		
Fuller John	E	1823	San Barbara	Butcher & Lighterman	M. D.
Fitch Henry D.	A		San Diego	Sea Captain, & Merchant	M. D
Foster John	E		Los Angeles	Merchant & Ranchero	M. L
Fling Guy F.	A	1831	Monterey	Blacksmith	L.
Fravel Ephraim	A	1834	San Jose	Tailor	L.
Frazer George	A		Sacramento	Trapper	L
Foxen Benjamin	E	1824	Santa Barbara	Shoemaker	
Furginson Daniel	E		Monterey	Laborer	M. D.
Farnham	A		Santa Cruz		D
Furginson Jesse	A				
Faxon William T.	A		Monterey	Storekeeper	D
Foster Charles	A				
Forbes James A.			San Jose	Merchant & Ranchero	M. L.
Flemming James	E		Monterey	Teamster	L.
Fuller Asiel	A				
Fippard Charles	A		M.	Lumberman	
Forsyth James	E		Monterey	"	
Fellum Math[e]w			Gilroy	Soap maker	
Gilroy John	S	1814	Gilroy	Miller & Soap Maker	M. L
Gale William A.	A	1824	Santa Barbara	Supercargo, Importer	M. D
Garner William R.	E	1824	Monterey	Lumberman, Trading	M. D.
Gulnac William	A	1832	San Jose	Blacksmith	M. D.
Graham Isaac	A	1836	Monterey	Disteller	L.
Greybatch William	E		Gilroy	Soap maker	D.
Gilbreth Isaac	A		Los Angeles	Carpenter	
German John	I		Monterey	Adobe Maker	G. D
Gardner Whyman	A	1839	do	Laborer	L
Goddard Lemuel		1833	Santa Barbara	Mariner	D

Persons Names	What Nation	Year of Arrival	Where Residing	Trade or Occupation	Married in California Marked M / Now living marked L / Dead marked D / Left Cal. Marked G
Hill Daniel	A	1823	Santa Barbara	Merchant & Ranchero	M. L
Hartnell William E. P.	E	1822	Monterey	Ranchero & Gov't Employee	M. D.
Charles Hall	A	1831	Santa Barbara	Store Keeper	D
Hall James	A	1834	San Francisco	Sea Captain	G. did not settle
Hitchcock Isaac	A	1832	Traveling	Trapping & Trading	G.
Hope Gerald	I		Monterey	Hatter	G
Hope John	A		do		
Hays Elias	A		do	Shingle Maker	G
Higgens John	I		Santa Cruz	Lumberman	D
Howard William D. M	A	1839	San Francisco	Supercargo	D
Hatherway Humphy	A	1839	Monterey	Carpenter	G
Hughes William O	A		do	Blacksmith	G
Hewett George	A				
Hemstead Sidney	A		Santa Barbara	Mariner	D
Hinckley William H.	A		San Francisco	Town officer & merchant	M. D.
House Thomas	I	1817	Sonoma	Mason	L.
Hill Leas	A	1823	Santa Barbara	Ranchero	D.
Hatch B. James	A	1835	On Board	Ship Master	D
Harrison David	A	1829	Santa Barbara	Mariner	D
Jones Jerimiah	E	1822	Sonoma	Mason	D.
Johnstone James	E		Los Angeles	Merchant & Ranchero	M. D
Jones John C.	A	1829	Santa Barbara	Ship owner, & Importer	M. L. G.
Jones Peter	A				
Jackson Edward	A				
Jinkins John					
Kenlock George	S	1829	Monterey	Cabinet Maker	M. L
Kenlock George Mrs.	S	1829	do		M. D.
Keith William M.	A	1832	Los Angeles	Physician	D.
King Robert	E		Santa Cruz	Lumberman	M. D.
Kennedy James	I				
Kelly Henry	A				

Persons Names	What Nation	Year of Arrival	Where Residing	Trade or Occupation	Married in California Marked M / Now living marked L / Dead marked D / Left Cal. Marked G
Littlejohn David	S	1823	Monterey	Dairy Man & Gardner	M. D.
Livermore Robert	E	1823	San Joaquin	Ranchero	M. L.
Lodge Michial	I		Santa Cruz	Miller, & Shingle maker	M. D.
Larkin Thomas O.	A	1832	Monterey	Merchant	M. L
Larkin Thomas O. Mrs.	A	1832	do		M. L.
Leese Jacob P	A		Sonoma	Town officer, & Ranchero	M. L.
Lauglin, Richard			Los Angeles	Carpenter	
Love James	E	1834	Los Angeles		
Lawson Peter	A		Sacramento	Ranchero & mountain guide	L
Leighton John B	A				
Loring Samuel	A				
Lewis Thomas	A				
Libbey Elliot	A	1839	San Luis	Sea Captain	D
Lucas John	E				D
McLane George					
Low James					
McKinley James	S	1824	Monterey	Merchant	M. L
McAllester Michial	I	1826	Monterey	Blacksmith	D.
Martin John	S	1825	Santa Clara	Carpinter	D
Martin John	E		San Raphael	Ranchero	L.
Mulligan John	I	1814	Monterey	do	D
Murphy Timothy	I	1829	San Raphael	do	D
Merrett Ezekial	A	1829	Sacramento	Trapper	D
Macondray John O.	E	A	1832	Monterey	Retailer	D
Majors Joseph L.	A		Santa Cruz	Lumberman & trading	M. L.
Mellus Henry	A	1835	Los Angeles	Supercargo	M. L. G.
Marsh John	A	1836	San Joaquin	Physician & Ranchero	D
McVickers Henry	A	1836	Monterey	Carpenter	L
Merrett Joseph	A	1832	Sacramento	Trapper	D
McFarland William					
McIntosh Edward	S		Monterey	Lumberman	L.
Merrell J.	A			Trapper	D

Persons Names	What Nation	Year of Arrival	Where Residing	Trade or Occupation	Married in California Marked M / Now living marked L / Dead marked D / Left Cal. Marked G
McCoon Perry	A	37		do	
Meadows James	E		Monterey	Herdsman	L.
McCarthy William	E		do	Teamster	
Mills John	E		do	Lumberman	
Matthus William	E		do	Teamster	M. L
McPherson James					
Miller Daniel	A			Herdsman	
McLean George					
Mellus Francis	A	1838	Los Angeles	Supercargo	M. L
Matthus John	E		Gilroy	Soaper Maker & Teamster	L
Mellish			Santa Cruz	Store Keeper	G.
Nidever George	A		Santa Barbara	Sea Otter Hunter & trading	L
Niele Henry	A	1836	Monterey	Disteller	D. Killed
Nye Gorham H	A	1829	San Francisco	Sea Captain	L.
Oliver John	E		Pajaro	Lumberman	G.
Owens Charles	A				
O'Brien James	I			Lumberman	
O'Brien John	I				
Prentis Samuel	A		Santa Barbara	Sea Otter Hunter	D.
Paty Henry	A	1833	Monterey	Ship Owner & Importer	D
Park Thomas B.	A		Santa Barbara	Supercargo	D.
Price John	A	1832	San Jose	Retailer	D.
Price John	E		Santa Cruz	Lumberman	M. L.
Plummer Henry	A				
Paty John	A	1837	San Francisco	Ship Owner, & Importer	L. G
Pickernell John	A		Monterey	Lumberman	M. D.
Prior M. Nathaniel	A	1828	Los Angeles		
Richardson William A	E	1822	San Francisco	Port Officer & Ranchero	M. D.
Rice George	A	1825	Los Angeles	Merchant	M. L. G.
Read John		1827	San Raphael	Ranchero	M. D

Persons Names	What Nation	Year of Arrival	Where Residing	Trade or Occupation	Married in California Marked M / Now living marked L / Dead marked D / Left Cal. Marked G
Reid Hugh		1834	Los Angeles	Writer & Vinyard	M. D.
Rhea John	A	1833	do	Merchant	G
Rhea Brother	A	18			
Runnals Stephen	E	18	Gilroy	Soap Maker	
Robbins Thomas M.	A	1823	Santa Barbara	Sea Captain & merchant	M. D.
Rainsford John	E		San Francisco	Lighterman	D
Rodgers James	E		Monterey	Teamster	M. D.
Roe Charles	A		do		
Richardson William	I		do	Tailor	M. L
Rollens John	I		Pajaro	Hewer	
Rice Isaac B.	A		do	Lumberman	
Ridley Robert T.	E		San Francisco	Town Officer, & Ranchero	M. D
Rightinson Thomas	A		Monterey		
Rumrill George W.	A		do	Blacksmith	G.
Robinson Alfred	A	1828	Santa Barbara	Supercargo, & Produce Exporter	M. L. G.
Spear Nathan	A	1823	San Francisco	Importer	D
Spence David	S	1824	Monterey	Merchant	M. L.
Stearns Abel	A	1829	Los Angeles	do	M. L.
Scott James	S	1826	Santa Barbara	Ship Owner & Importer	D.
Stone Daniel	A	1832	San Jose	R	
Sinclair Prumet	A	1832	Santa Barbara	Sea Otter Hunter	D
Smith Jedidiah	A	1829	Traveling	Trapper & Trading	
Sill Daniel	A	1831	San Francisco	Millwright	L
Smith Charles	A	1831	Monterey	Importer	L
Stevens	A		San Diego	Sea Captain, Sea Otter Hunter	L
Stevens Mrs	A		San Diego		L
Smith John	E		Monterey	Carpenter	L
Scott James	E		Pajaro	Lumberman	G.
Stevens John					
Smith	A		Sonoma	Sea Captain	D
Simmons Stephen	A		Santa Barbara	Sea Otter Hunter	
Smith William		1812	Santa Barbara	Sea Captain	D
Slade Oliver	A		Monterey	Carpenter	G.

Persons Names	What Nation	Year of Arrival	Where Residing	Trade or Occupation	Married in California Marked M / Now living marked L / Dead marked D / Left Cal. Marked G
Snooks Joseph	E	29	San Diego	Sea Captain	M. D
Sparks Isaac	A	1833	Santa Barbara	Sea Otter Hunter & Trading	M. L.
Southard Eli	A		San Francisco	Carpenter	L
Shields Samuel					
Stetson Edward L.	A	1839	Monterey	Writer	L. G.
Stokes James	E	1833	Monterey	Merchant & Druggist	M. L.
Spaulding Joseph	A				
Smith Jedidiah Capt.	A	1829	First company overland	Trapping & Trading	D. Killed
Shaw Thomas	A		On Board	Supercargo	D
Saunders William	A				
Thompson William	E	1822	Santa Cruz	Lumberman	M. L
Thompson Samuel	E		do	do	M. L.
Thompson	S	1824	Santa Barbara	Shoe Maker	
Tevy	S	1825	Monterey	Butcher & Packer	
Temple John	A	1825	Los Angeles	Merchant	M. L
Thompson Thomas	A				
Trevethan William	E	1824	Monterey	Lumberman	L
Tomlinson Thomas A.	A		do	Hatter	M. D
Thomas Thomas	E	1838			D
Trask George					
Thompson Joseph P.	A	1839	San Francisco	Supercargo	L
Thompson Alpheus B.	A	1829	Santa Barbara	Ship Owner, & Importer	M. L.
Young Levy Capt.	A	1833	Traveling	Trapper & Trading	D.
Yount George	A	1831	Napa	Miller, & Ranchero	L. M.
Young Francis	E		Santa Cruz	Lumberman	M. L.
Vincent George W.	A	1826	San Francisco	Sea Captain	D.
Watson James	E	1824	Monterey	Merchant	M. L.
Wilson John	S	1825	San Luis Obispo	Sea Captain & Ship owner	M. L.

Persons Names	What Nation	Year of Arrival	Where Residing	Trade or Occupation	Married in California Marked M / Now living marked L / Dead marked D / Left Cal. Marked G
Wilson William	A	1821	San Jose	Laborer	D
Welsh William		1824	San Joaquin	Ranchero	M. D.
Weeks James	E		San Jose	Town officer	M. L.
Walker Joseph	A	1833	Traveling	Trapping & Trading	L.
West William M	E	1829	Monterey	Carpenter	M. D.
Warner John T.	A		Los Angeles	Merchant & Ranchero	M. L
Wolfskill William	A		do	Vinyard & Orchard	M. L
Wolfskill John	A		do	do	L.
Watson Edward	E		Monterey	Store Keeper	M. D.
Ware William	I	1832	Santa Cruz	Lumberman	
Williams Isaac	A	1833	Los Angeles	Merchant & Ranchero	M. D.
Webb William	A		Monterey	Carpenter	G.
Warren William R.	A	38	do	Store Keeping	D.
White Michael	E				
Wilson Alvin	A		Monterey	Laborer	
Wood Henry	A		Traveling	Mountain Guide	L
Williams George	E		Santa Cruz	Laborer	
Warren Cornelius	A		do	do	
Whitton Ezekiel	A		Monterey	do	
Whitton Jeremiah	A		do	do	
Warren Henry	A		do	do	
Woodworth John	A		do	do	
Whitmarsh	A	1836	Sonoma	Tailor	
Williams Benjamin	A	1836		Laborer	L.
Watson Andrew	E		Monterey	Carpenter	M. L.
Williamson Thomas	A		do	Laborer	
Wyman Gardner	A		do	Herdsman	
Whyman F. George	A	1836	Santa Cruz	Lumberman	
Wilson Benj[n]	A	1840	Los Angeles	Merchant	L M

INDEX

The Appendix has not been included in this Index.